An Introduction to Discussion Skills

GLOBAL ISSUES

Garry Pearson   **Graham Skerritt**   **Adrian Francis**   **Hiroshi YOSHIZUKA**

JN062939

SEIBIDO

音声ファイルのダウンロード／ストリーミング

🔊 マーク表示がある箇所は、音声を弊社 HP より無料でダウンロード／ストリーミングすることができます。下記 URL の書籍詳細ページに音声ダウンロードアイコンがございますのでそちらから自習用音声としてご活用ください。

http://seibido.co.jp/ad598

Global Issues

Preface

After teaching discussion skills both at universities in Japan and at Global Bridge (one of Japan's leading corporate training companies), we want to share the approach we have used successfully with our students.

By teaching the skills and phrases that students need to take part in discussions, *Global Issues* helps you to develop your ability to have proper discussions—an essential skill to learn both for academic work and for your future careers.

As the title suggests, *Global Issues* focuses on a range of problems facing the world and how different countries are trying to solve them. For example, we look at how France is tackling environmental problems caused by fast fashion, at how South Korea has attempted to deal with online bullying over social media, and how education in Finland is getting better results than other countries.

We hope that you enjoy discussing these topics as much as our students have.

Garry Pearson, Graham Skerritt, Adrian Francis and Hiroshi Yoshizuka

Acknowledgements

We would like to thank Mr. Eiichi Tamura and Mr. Taiichi Sano at Seibido for their support and guidance while writing this book.

Contents

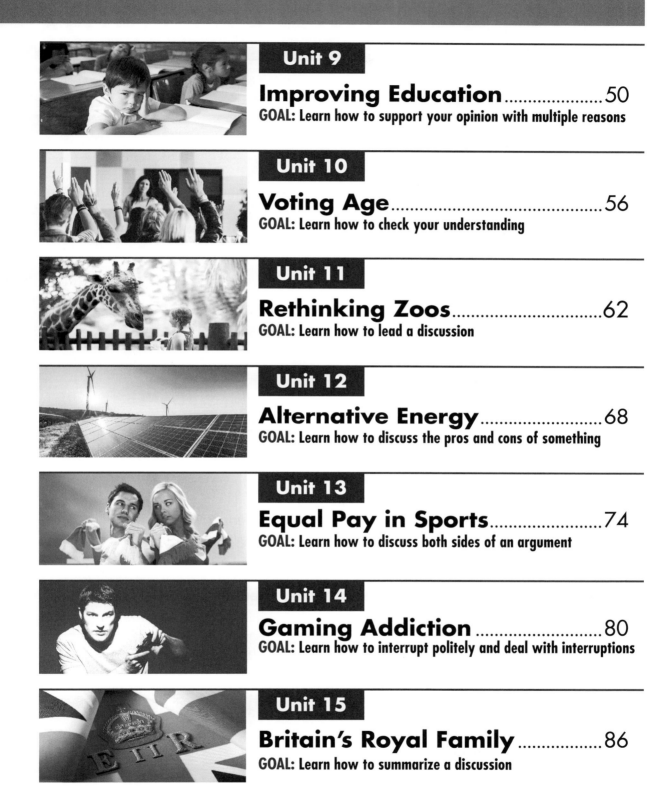

Unit 1
The Cashless Society

GOAL: Learn how to discuss opinions

GET READY

1 **Discuss these questions with a partner.**

▷ How often do you pay for things with cash?
▷ When do you use cashless payments?
▷ Do you prefer using cash or making cashless payments? Why?

VOCABULARY

2 🔊 1-2 **Read and listen to the sentences. Then match the words in bold to the definitions below.**

> **1.** I couldn't pay because the shop didn't **accept** credit cards. ___
> **2.** I used this **app** on my phone to check my credit card balance. ___
> **3.** I accidentally ripped a $10 **bill**, so I fixed it with tape. ___
> **4.** I don't like carrying **coins** because they're so heavy! ___
> **5.** These days most **purchases** are done online. ___
> **6.** I only **withdraw** money from an ATM once per week. ___

a. paper money
b. take money out of a bank
c. a computer program, often for cell phones
d. agree to take something as payment
e. small, round pieces of metal that are used as money
f. payments to buy things

LISTENING

3 🔊 1-3, 4 **Read the listening tip. Listen and repeat the example sentences.**

LISTENING TIP: Dropping *t* and *d* at the end of words

Speakers often don't say *t* or *d* sounds at the end of a word when the next word starts with a consonant sound.

1. I couldn'(t) pay because the shop didn't accep(t) credi(t) cards.
2. I use(d) this app on my phone to check my credi(t) car(d) balance.

4 🔊 1-5～7 **Listen and write the missing words. Then listen and repeat.**

1. I went to the bank _____ _____ but it _____ _____ I got there.

2. That cafe wouldn't ____ ____ use my card so I went to the cafe _____ _____.

3. I wish I _____ ____ for more things with my _____ ____.

◆ LISTEN FOR MAIN IDEAS:

5 🔊 1-8 **Listen and choose the best summary of the report.**

❏ **a.** All countries will probably be cashless soon.
❏ **b.** Sweden is going cashless, but most Swedish people are unhappy about this.
❏ **c.** Sweden may become cashless soon, but some countries are not ready yet.

◆ LISTEN FOR DETAILS:

6 🔊 1-8 **Listen again and choose the correct answers.**

1. What percentage of payments are cashless in Sweden?
❏ **a.** 80%
❏ **b.** 40%
❏ **c.** 20%

2. Where can people not use cash in Sweden?
❏ **a.** shops
❏ **b.** ATMs
❏ **c.** trains

3. According to the report, what is one reason that cash is still popular in Japan?
❏ **a.** Because people don't think cashless payments are safe.
❏ **b.** Because there isn't much crime.
❏ **c.** Because it's faster than cashless payments.

A Cashless Society?

Sweden may become the [1]_____ _____ to go cashless. In fact, some experts think that this could happen in the [2]_____ _____ years.

In Sweden, 80% of all purchases are made [3]_____ _____. Swedish people buy things with credit cards, debit cards, and an app called Swish. As a result, some businesses in Sweden have stopped taking cash. Buses [4]_____ _____ in Stockholm no longer accept coins or bills, several ATMs have been shut down, and many shops have signs that say "No cash payments."

However, not all countries are changing as quickly as Sweden. In Japan, only 20% of purchases are cashless. One reason is that there [5]_____ _____ crime, so people feel safe withdrawing cash from ATMs and carrying it in their wallets.

So, although Sweden is [6]_____ _____ to go cashless, other countries are not ready to change yet.

CONVERSATION

◆ BEFORE YOU LISTEN:

8 Look at these sentences. Which ones are reasons for going cashless, and which are reasons against going cashless?

	for	against
1. Cashiers would not make mistakes with change.		
2. Small shops would have to buy expensive new cash registers.		
3. Carrying lots of money around in your wallet is not safe.		
4. People can get sick from touching money.		
5. Elderly people don't know how to use apps to pay for things.		
6. The government could check how people use their money and that they are paying the correct amount of tax.		
7. People would have no privacy, because computers would record all the items that they bought.		
8. Shops couldn't sell things if there was a problem with the technology.		

◆ LISTEN FOR MAIN IDEAS:

9 🔊 1-9 **Listen to a conversation between Tomoko and Marcus. Do they think that the world should go cashless?**

    1. Marcus thinks that the world should / shouldn't go cashless.

    2. Tomoko thinks that the world should / shouldn't go cashless.

◆ LISTEN FOR DETAILS:

10 🔊 1-9 **Listen again. Which reasons from Activity 8 do they give for their opinions? Write the number of the reason.**

    1. Marcus _____

    2. Tomoko _____

11 Work in pairs. Practice the conversation.

Asking for an opinion →

Tomoko: Do you think the world should become cashless?

1. _____ →

Marcus: I strongly believe that it shouldn't as small shops would have to buy expensive new cash registers.

2. _____ →

Tomoko: That's a good point.

Marcus: What do you think?

Tomoko: I think the world should become cashless because carrying lots of money around in my wallet is not safe.

Marcus: I see what you mean.

DISCUSSION

12 🔊 1-10 **Look at the chart. Add labels to the conversation on page 6. Then practice saying the phrases in the chart.**

💬 **DISCUSSION SKILL:** Discussing opinions	
Asking for an opinion	· **Do you think** the world should become cashless? · **What do you think?** · **What's your opinion?**
Giving an opinion and a reason	· **I strongly believe that** it shouldn't become cashless **as** shops would have to buy new cash registers. · **I think that** the world should become cashless **because** carrying lots of money is not safe. · **I'm not sure, but perhaps** the world shouldn't become cashless **since** people would have no privacy.
Reacting	· **I see.** · **That's a good point.** · **I see what you mean.**

13 **Discuss this question with your partner: *Should Japan become cashless?* Use the phrases in Activity 12 and the diagram below to help you.**

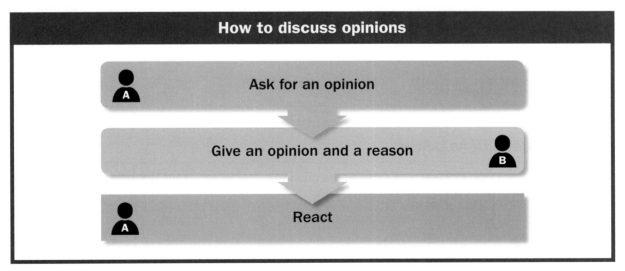

How to discuss opinions

A → Ask for an opinion

Give an opinion and a reason ← B

A → React

A: Some people think that Japan should go cashless. What do you think?
B: I think that …

Fast Fashion

GOAL: Learn how to ask questions if you didn't hear or understand

GET READY

1 **Discuss these questions with a partner.**

▷ How often do you buy clothes?
▷ What's most important when you buy clothes: price, style, brand, or something else?
▷ Do you ever throw clothes away?

VOCABULARY

2 🔊 **1-11** **Read and listen to the sentences. Then match the words in bold to the definitions below.**

1. Factories produce a lot of **carbon emissions** that are bad for the environment. ___
2. My sister works for a **charity** on Park Street that helps sick people. ___
3. I've decided to **donate** some old clothes to a used clothing store. ___
4. Things that can't be recycled are often taken to **a landfill**. ___
5. That factory is owned by a clothes **manufacturer**. ___
6. I think it's time to **replace** my jeans—they have holes in them. ___

   a. CO_2 gas made by cars, trucks, etc.
   b. a place where trash is buried in the ground
   c. give
   d. an organization that helps people who are in need
   e. throw out something and get a new one
   f. a company that makes something

LISTENING

3 🔊 1-12, 13 **Read the listening tip. Listen and repeat the example sentences.**

LISTENING TIP: Linking with y

When one word ends with **y** and the next word starts with a vowel, the words link with a **y** sound.

1. That factor<u>y is</u> owned by a clothes manufacturer.
2. My sister works for a charit<u>y on</u> Park Street that helps sick people.

4 🔊 1-14~16 **Listen and write the missing words. Then listen and repeat the sentences.**

1. A new clothing store has _____ _____ in my town.

2. These clothes are _____ _____ fashionable.

3. My friend is _____ _____ that I didn't recycle my old clothes.

◆ **LISTEN FOR MAIN IDEAS:**

5 🔊 1-17 **Listen to the report and choose the best summary.**

❑ **a.** The popularity of fast fashion has increased clothes production and therefore increased damage to the environment.

❑ **b.** The popularity of fast fashion has changed clothes production so that it is better for the environment.

❑ **c.** The popularity of fast fashion has caused people to donate more items to charity.

◆ **LISTEN FOR DETAILS:**

6 🔊 1-17 **Listen again and complete the sentences.**

1. The fashion industry is responsible for _____ of the world's carbon emissions.

2. The fashion industry causes _____ of water pollution around the world.

3. _____ of the clothes produced go into landfills each year.

4. A new law in France says that companies cannot destroy or _____ _____ unsold goods or clothes.

Fighting Fast Fashion

In recent years, fast fashion has become very popular. Many clothes manufacturers now produce cheap, ¹_____ _____ that people wear for a short time and then replace. The ²_____ ____ this approach has doubled clothes production since the year 2000.

However, this is bad news for the environment. The fashion ³_____ ___ responsible for 10% of the world's carbon emissions and causes 20% of water pollution around the world. In addition, 85% of the clothes produced go into landfills each year. And, shockingly, most of these items come from shops that throw away clothes that nobody bought.

So, what can be done about this problem? One solution may be a new law ⁴_____ _____ in France. According to this law, companies are not allowed to ⁵_____ ____ throw away unsold goods. It is hoped that this will encourage companies to produce fewer items and donate more products to charity.

CONVERSATION

◆ BEFORE YOU LISTEN:

8 Match the halves of these sentences.

Arguments for fast fashion

1. It means that poorer people can ...

2. It allows people to easily change ...

3. It helps shops keep up to date ...

4. It creates more ...

5. It makes shopping fun because there are always ...

a. new things to see. ___

b. buy more clothes. ___

c. their style. ___

d. with the latest trends. ___

e. jobs for people. ___

Arguments against fast fashion

6. It's bad for ...

7. It causes people to ...

8. It encourages manufacturers to produce ...

9. It means that manufacturers can pay low wages to ...

10. It's actually more expensive than buying ...

f. low-quality products. ___

g. throw away more clothes. ___

h. the environment. ___

i. people in poor countries. ___

j. a few high-quality items. ___

◆ LISTEN FOR MAIN IDEAS:

9 🔊 1-18 Listen to a conversation between Kenzo and Tam. Answer the questions.

1. Does Tam think that fast fashion should be banned?

2. Which reason from Activity 8 does she give for her opinion?

◆ LISTEN FOR DETAILS:

10 🔊 1-18 Listen again and answer the questions.

1. Why couldn't Kenzo hear Tam?

2. What word didn't Kenzo understand?

3. Did Kenzo understand Tam's explanation of the word?

11 Work in pairs. Practice the conversation.

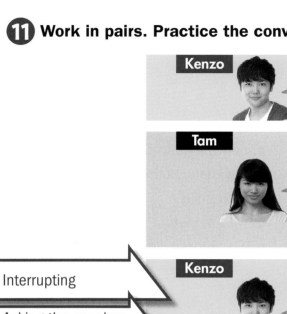

Kenzo: So, do you think fast fashion should be banned?

Tam: Yes, I strongly believe that it should, because it encourages manufacturers to produce low-quality products that people wear a couple of times and then throw away. I think—

Interrupting

Asking the speaker to say something again

Kenzo: I'm sorry to interrupt, but I didn't hear you. Could you speak a little louder, please?

Tam: Sure. I said that I believe fast fashion should be banned as it encourages companies to make low-quality items that people only wear once or twice and then throw away. It's really wasteful.

Interrupting

Asking the speaker to explain something

Kenzo: Sorry, but what does "wasteful" mean?

Tam: Oh, being wasteful means throwing something away without using it much. People worked hard to make these clothes, so we shouldn't throw them away so quickly.

Kenzo: Okay. I got it. Yes, that's a good point.

Tam: So, what do you think? Should fast fashion be banned?

DISCUSSION

12 🔊 1-19 **Look at the chart. Underline the phrases in the conversation on page 12 that Kenzo uses. Then practice saying the phrases in the chart.**

💬 DISCUSSION SKILL: Asking questions if you didn't hear or understand		
Interrupting	· Sorry, but … · Excuse me … · I'm sorry to interrupt, but …	
Asking the speaker to say something again	I didn't hear you.	· Could you repeat that, please? · Could you speak a little slower, please? · Could you speak a little louder, please? · Did you say "15" or "50"?
Asking the speaker to explain something	I don't understand.	· What does "wasteful" mean? · Could you reword that for me, please?

13 **Discuss this question with your partner:** *Should the government ban fast fashion?* **Use the phrases in Activity 12 and the diagram below to help you.**

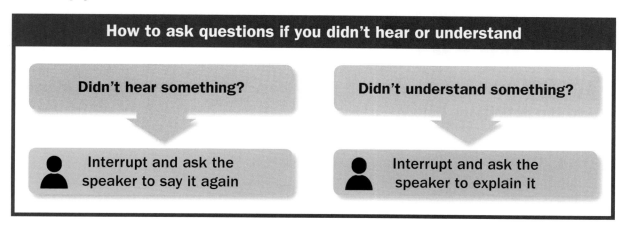

How to ask questions if you didn't hear or understand
Didn't hear something?   **Didn't understand something?**
⬇   ⬇
👤 Interrupt and ask the speaker to say it again   👤 Interrupt and ask the speaker to explain it

A: Do you think fast fashion should be banned?
B: I think that …

Plastic Packaging

GOAL: Learn how to agree and disagree

GET READY

1 **Discuss these questions with a partner.**

▷ What are some environmental problems?
▷ How often do you use plastic products?
▷ How can people reduce the amount of plastic they use?

VOCABULARY

2 🔊 1-20 **Read and listen to the sentences. Then match the words in bold to the definitions below.**

> **1.** Because of email, there's been **a decline** in the use of paper. ___
> **2.** The coronavirus had a **devastating** impact on tourism. ___
> **3.** Instead of **disposable** chopsticks, restaurants should use washable ones. ___
> **4.** Our university has very modern **facilities**, such as a gym and cafeteria. ___
> **5.** I can't believe that some people drop **trash** on the ground, not in a garbage can. ___
> **6.** Factories that manufacture products often produce a large amount of **waste**. ___

a. used once or twice and then thrown away
b. a decrease
c. garbage
d. something leftover or unused after production
e. places or equipment used for a special purpose
f. damaging or destructive

LISTENING

3 🔊 1-21, 22 **Read the listening tip. Listen and repeat the example sentences.**

LISTENING TIP: Sentence stress

The most important words in each sentence are stressed (said more loudly and clearly than other words). If you focus on these, you can understand the basic meaning.

1. Because of **email**, there's been a **decline** in the use of **paper**.
2. The **coronavirus** had a **devastating impact** on **tourism**.

4 🔊 1-23~25 **Listen and write the missing words. Then listen and repeat the sentences.**

1. The **biggest environmental problem** we have is _____.
2. I think we should _____ **using plastic bags** at the **supermarket**.
3. **I don't like seeing** _____ in **forests** and **rivers**.

◆ **LISTEN FOR MAIN IDEAS:**

5 🔊 1-26 **Listen to the report and choose the correct answers.**

1. How much plastic waste does Indonesia produce?
❏ **a.** more than any country in the world
❏ **b.** more than China
❏ **c.** more than any other country besides China

2. How does the Indonesian government plan to become a plastic-free country?
❏ **a.** by closing waste disposal facilities
❏ **b.** by banning fishing nets
❏ **c.** by taxing manufacturers of plastic products

◆ **LISTEN FOR DETAILS:**

6 🔊 1-26 **Listen again and decide if each sentence is true or false.**

1. Indonesian people often use disposable plastic items. T/F
2. Almost 15% of plastic waste in the world's oceans is from Indonesia. T/F
3. The number of fish caught has increased. T/F
4. The government plans to make Indonesia plastic-free by 2040. T/F

Indonesia's Problem with Plastic

Indonesia has a plastic problem. After ¹_____ , it produces more plastic waste than any other nation. Because plastic is ²_____ and easy to produce, many everyday items, such as knives and forks, are ³_____ —used once and then thrown away.

The environmental impact has been devastating. In fact, almost ⁴_____ of plastic waste in the world's oceans comes from Indonesia. Many of its ⁵_____ are now covered by a layer of trash. The ⁶_____ are filled with plastic too, which often gets trapped in fishing nets and has led to a decline in the number of fish caught.

The issue is so serious that the government has announced plans for a plastic-free Indonesia by ⁷_____. They plan to achieve this goal by taxing the ⁸_____ of products that use plastic, as well as building ⁹_____ and waste disposal facilities.

The government hopes that ending plastic waste will see the return of the beautiful beaches the country was once famous for.

CONVERSATION

◆ BEFORE YOU LISTEN:

8 Look at these sentences. Which ones are reasons for going plastic-free and which are reasons against going plastic-free?

	for	against
1. It's not possible to stop using plastic completely.		
2. Plastic waste has a devastating impact on sea creatures.		
3. Making plastic damages the environment.		
4. Plastic bags are difficult to recycle.		
5. It would encourage companies to develop green packaging.		
6. Disposable items are very convenient.		
7. Plastic products, such as furniture, can be used for a long time.		
8. A total ban would be hard to enforce.		
9. It's traditional in Japan to have many layers of packaging.		
10. We don't need to wrap fruit and vegetables in plastic.		

◆ LISTEN FOR MAIN IDEAS:

9 🔊 1-27 Listen to a conversation between Yui and Mohammed. Answer the questions.

1. Does Yui think that plastic should be banned?

2. Which reason from Activity 8 does she give for her opinion?

◆ LISTEN FOR DETAILS:

10 🔊 1-27 Listen again. What does Yui think the government should do?

❏ **a.** ban supermarkets from wrapping fruit and vegetables

❏ **b.** announce a complete ban on plastic

❏ **c.** develop green packaging

11 Work in pairs. Practice the conversation.

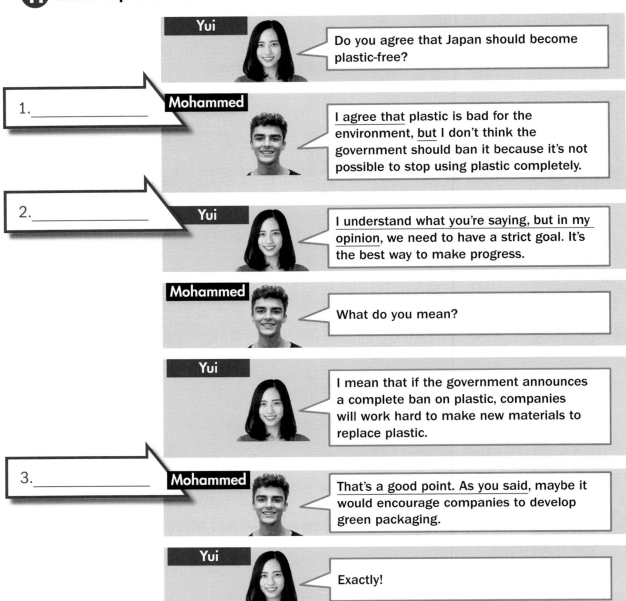

Yui: Do you agree that Japan should become plastic-free?

1._____

Mohammed: I agree that plastic is bad for the environment, but I don't think the government should ban it because it's not possible to stop using plastic completely.

2._____

Yui: I understand what you're saying, but in my opinion, we need to have a strict goal. It's the best way to make progress.

Mohammed: What do you mean?

Yui: I mean that if the government announces a complete ban on plastic, companies will work hard to make new materials to replace plastic.

3._____

Mohammed: That's a good point. As you said, maybe it would encourage companies to develop green packaging.

Yui: Exactly!

DISCUSSION

12 🔊 1-28 **Look at the chart. Add the labels to the conversation on page 18. Then practice saying the phrases in the chart.**

💬 DISCUSSION SKILL: Agreeing and disagreeing	
Agreeing	• **I agree. As you said**, making plastic damages the environment. • **I think so too. Adding to what you said,** I think disposable items are very convenient. • **That's a good point.** • **Exactly!**
Partially agreeing	• **I partially agree, but** I don't think it's possible to stop using plastic completely. • **I agree that** plastic is bad for the environment, **but** I don't think the government should ban it.
Disagreeing politely	• **That's a good point, but** I think 2040 is too soon. • **I understand what you're saying, but** in my opinion, we need to have a strict goal.

13 **Discuss this question with your partner: *Should Japan become plastic free?* Use the phrases in Activity 12 and the diagram below to help you.**

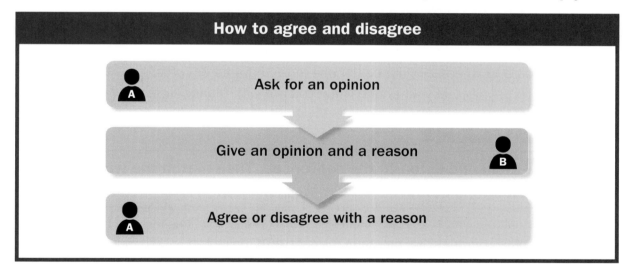

How to agree and disagree

A → Ask for an opinion

Give an opinion and a reason ← B

A → Agree or disagree with a reason

A: *Do you think Japan should become plastic free?*
B: *I believe that …*

Cell Phone Etiquette

GOAL: Learn how to give yourself time to think

GET READY

1 Discuss these questions with a partner.

▷ How often do you make or receive calls on your cell phone?
▷ Do you ever speak on your cell phone in restaurants or cafes?
▷ Do you usually use your phone when you are with friends or family members?

VOCABULARY

2 🔊 1-29 **Read and listen to the sentences. Then match the words in bold to the definitions below.**

> **1.** Restaurants with a great **atmosphere** always have people laughing and talking. ___
> **2.** In some countries, it's **common** for people to make phone calls on trains. ___
> **3.** I turn off my cell phone at work so I don't get **distracted** by messages. ___
> **4.** Public places like restaurants and museums should **restrict** cell phone use. ___
> **5.** I feel **satisfied** after a good meal and great conversation. ___
> **6.** I don't like rules that are too **strict**. ___

a. mood or feeling
b. interested in other things when trying to do a task
c. pleased or happy with something
d. only allow certain things
e. often done or happening
f. controlling

LISTENING

3 🔊 1-30, 31 **Read the listening tip. Listen and repeat the example sentences.**

LISTENING TIP: Consonant clusters

A consonant cluster is two or more consonants together in a word. There are no vowel sounds between these letters. Some common consonant clusters are *cl, sm, sp, st, str* and *tr*.

1. In some coun<u>tr</u>ies, it's common for people to make phone calls on <u>tr</u>ains.
2. Public places like re<u>st</u>aurants and museums should re<u>str</u>ict cell phone use.

4 🔊 1-32, 33 **Listen and write the missing words. Then listen and repeat the sentences.**

1. _____ call the _____ if there are any problems.
2. Coaches _____ people who play _____.

◆ LISTEN FOR MAIN IDEAS:

5 🔊 1-34 **Listen to the report and choose the correct answers.**

1. Why are some restaurant owners taking action to restrict cell phone use?
   - ❑ **a.** Because people who use their phones often don't order many dishes.
   - ❑ **b.** Because people who check their phones eat too slowly.
   - ❑ **c.** Because phones are not good for their restaurant's atmosphere.

2. What do the restaurant owners want customers to do?
   - ❑ **a.** share their restaurant reviews on social media
   - ❑ **b.** eat silently so they don't disturb other customers
   - ❑ **c.** enjoy their meal and conversation

◆ LISTEN FOR DETAILS:

6 🔊 1-34 **Listen again and choose the correct answers.**

1. According to the report, 70% of <u>adults</u> / <u>teenagers</u> feel that they should respond to messages immediately.
2. The number of restaurant owners who are restricting cell phone use is <u>increasing</u> / <u>decreasing</u>.
3. Customers who don't use their cell phones are <u>more</u> / <u>less</u> satisfied with their experience.

Phones Not Welcome!

These days it's common to see couples or families eating at a restaurant without ¹_____ to each other. The reason is they are too
²_____ by their cell phones. Recent studies show that 50% of adults and 70% of teenagers feel the need to ³_____ to messages immediately.

A ⁴_____ number of restaurant owners in New York think that things have gone too far. And these owners are trying different ways to
⁵_____ cell phone use. Some suggest ⁶_____ put away their phones, or offer discounts to people who leave them at home. But others have ⁷_____ a complete ban on phones in their restaurants.

These owners all believe that cell phones have ruined the atmosphere in their restaurants. ⁸_____, they want people to focus on enjoying food and conversation. After all, restaurants are for social connections, not social media.

Although these bans are ⁹_____, they seem to be working. Many of these
¹⁰_____ are busier than ever, and the customers themselves say they are more satisfied with the experience of dining out.

CONVERSATION

◆ BEFORE YOU LISTEN:

8 Rank these reasons for banning cell phones in restaurants from weakest (1) to strongest (5). Then rank the reasons against banning cell phones.

Reasons for banning cell phones in restaurants

a. People are more satisfied if they talk and laugh with others. _____

b. If everyone is using their phones, it ruins the atmosphere. _____

c. It's rude to focus on your phone instead of the people you are with. _____

d. Everybody needs to have a break from their phone. _____

e. The noise from phones might bother other customers. _____

Reasons against banning cell phones in restaurants

f. Paying customers should be able to do what they want. _____

g. Sending messages in a restaurant doesn't usually disturb other people . _____

h. If there's an emergency, not having a phone can be dangerous. _____

i. Many people eat alone so they need some entertainment while they eat. _____

j. It's possible to enjoy talking with others and use your phone at the same time.

_____

◆ LISTEN FOR MAIN IDEAS:

9 🔊 1-35 **Listen to a conversation between Max and Hana. Choose the correct word to complete the sentences.**

1. Max thinks that phones <u>should</u> / <u>shouldn't</u> be banned in restaurants.

2. Hana believes that restricting phone use in some places is <u>okay</u> / <u>not okay</u>.

◆ LISTEN FOR DETAILS:

10 🔊 1-35 **Listen again. Which reasons from Activity 8 do Max and Hana give for their opinions?**

1. Max _____

2. Hana _____

23

11 **Work in pairs. Practice the conversation.**

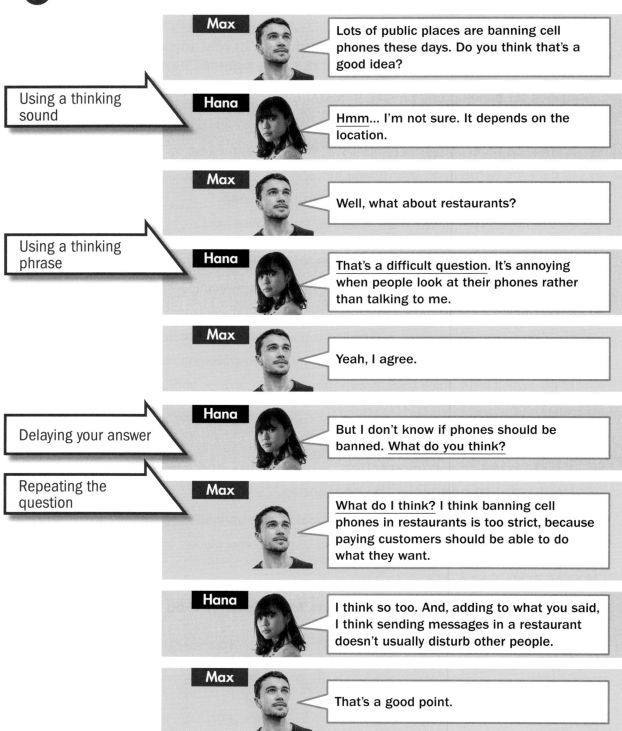

Max: Lots of public places are banning cell phones these days. Do you think that's a good idea?

Using a thinking sound

Hana: Hmm... I'm not sure. It depends on the location.

Max: Well, what about restaurants?

Using a thinking phrase

Hana: That's a difficult question. It's annoying when people look at their phones rather than talking to me.

Max: Yeah, I agree.

Delaying your answer

Hana: But I don't know if phones should be banned. What do you think?

Repeating the question

Max: What do I think? I think banning cell phones in restaurants is too strict, because paying customers should be able to do what they want.

Hana: I think so too. And, adding to what you said, I think sending messages in a restaurant doesn't usually disturb other people.

Max: That's a good point.

DISCUSSION

12 🔊 1-36 Check (✓) the sounds and phrases that Max and Hana use in the conversation on page 24. Which question does Max repeat? Then practice saying the phrases in the chart.

💬 DISCUSSION SKILL: Giving yourself time to think	
Using a thinking sound	❑ **Hmm** ❑ **Uh** ❑ **Um**
Using a thinking phrase	❑ **Let me think.** ❑ **That's a good question.** ❑ **That's a difficult question.** ❑ **I've never thought about that before.**
Repeating the question	❑ *"What should they do?"* → What should they do? ❑ *"What do you think?"* → What do *I* think?
Delaying your answer	❑ **What do you think?** ❑ **Can you come back to me?**

13 Discuss this question with your partner: *Should cell phones be banned in the locations below?* Use the phrases in Activity 12 and the diagram below to help you.

- in schools
- in university classes
- in restaurants
- in cinemas
- on buses and trains
- at work
- in meetings
- in cars
- in parks

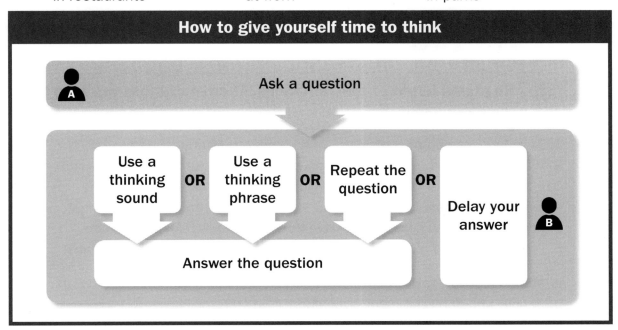

How to give yourself time to think

A Ask a question

Use a thinking sound **OR** Use a thinking phrase **OR** Repeat the question **OR** Delay your answer B

Answer the question

A: Some people think that cell phones should be banned in public places. What do you think?
B: Hmm. I'm not sure, but perhaps ...

Vegetarianism

GET READY

1 **Discuss these questions with a partner.**

▷ What animals do people often eat?
▷ How often do you eat meat?
▷ Why do some people choose not to eat meat?

VOCABULARY

2 🔊 1-37 **Read and listen to the sentences. Then match the words in bold to the definitions below.**

> **1.** To reduce my **carbon footprint**, I'm not going to fly on planes. ___
> **2.** Actually, eating less meat is a good way to **contribute** to a greener world. ___
> **3.** I don't think meat is necessary to get enough **nutrition**. ___
> **4.** In general, **a plant-based diet** is better for your health than eating meat. ___
> **5.** I don't think I could become **a vegan** because I love milk and cheese. ___
> **6.** I strongly believe restaurants should offer more options for **vegetarians**. ___

a. someone who doesn't eat meat, seafood or animal products
b. people who don't eat meat or seafood
c. a diet that includes no meat
d. food for health and growth
e. the amount of CO_2 one person is responsible for
f. help by giving or doing something

LISTENING

3 🔊 1-38, 39 **Read the listening tip. Listen and repeat the example sentences.**

LISTENING TIP: Signpost words

Speakers use signpost words to tell listeners about what's coming next. For example, they can be used to show that the speaker is going to add another point (*in addition, also*), provide some contrasting information (*however, actually*) or give an example (*for example*). Signpost words are often stressed.

   1. <u>Actually</u>, eating less meat is a good way to contribute to a greener world.
   2. <u>In general</u>, a plant-based diet is better for your health than eating meat.

4 🔊 1-40~43 **Listen and write the missing words. Then listen and repeat the sentences.**

   1. _____ _____, many forests are being cut down in Brazil.
   2. _____, it's not the only way to help the environment.
   3. _____, people should stop using so much plastic.
   4. ___ _____, they can recycle paper and glass.

◆ **LISTEN FOR MAIN IDEAS:**

5 🔊 1-44 **Listen to the report and choose the best summary.**

   ❏ **a.** People choose plant-based diets for a variety of reasons.
   ❏ **b.** The number of vegetarians and vegans is decreasing.
   ❏ **c.** More people are choosing plant-based diets for environmental reasons.

◆ **LISTEN FOR DETAILS:**

6 🔊 1-44 **Listen again and choose the correct answers.**

   1. What percentage of people in New Zealand are vegetarian or vegan?
      ❏ **a.** over 15%
      ❏ **b.** over 50%
      ❏ **c.** over 0.15%

   2. In the past, many people gave up meat because...
      ❏ **a.** they thought it was unhealthy.
      ❏ **b.** they thought it was wrong to kill animals for food.
      ❏ **c.** they thought it was bad for the environment.

   3. According to the speaker, what will happen in the future?
      ❏ **a.** The number of vegans and vegetarians will probably increase.
      ❏ **b.** The number of vegans and vegetarians will probably decrease.
      ❏ **c.** The number of vegans and vegetarians will probably stay the same.

The End of Meat?

In recent years, New Zealand has seen a large increase in the popularity of plant-based diets. ¹___ _____, more than 15% of the population is now either vegetarian or vegan. So what are the reasons behind this trend?

In the past, many people chose a plant-based diet because they thought it was wrong to kill animals for food, or because animals were treated poorly in meat production. But these days, the most significant reason for giving up meat is the environment. ²_____, eating meat may contribute the largest part of our individual carbon footprint. This is because the animals produce a huge amount of CO_2. ³_____ _____ is that forests are often cut down to make space for farmland.

⁴_____ _____, most people continue to eat meat—either because they enjoy the taste, or because they think it's important for nutrition. Convenience is also a factor, as most restaurants serve a limited range of vegetarian dishes. ⁵_____, as concern about the environment grows, the trend toward plant-based diets is likely to continue.

CONVERSATION

◆ BEFORE YOU LISTEN:

8 Rank these reasons for eating meat from weakest (1) to strongest (5). Then rank the reasons against eating meat.

Reasons for eating meat

a. It's delicious. _____

b. It has a lot of nutrition we need. _____

c. Most restaurants serve a limited range of vegetarian dishes. _____

d. It's natural for people to eat meat. _____

e. Meat is good for brain development. _____

Reasons against eating meat

f. Meat can be unhealthy. _____

g. Animals raised for meat are treated poorly. _____

h. It's wrong to kill animals for food. _____

i. Animals produce too much CO_2. _____

j. Farmers cut down forests to make space for farming animals. _____

◆ LISTEN FOR MAIN IDEAS:

9 🔊 1-45 Listen to a conversation between Simone and Nao. Answer the questions.

1. Does Nao think people should eat meat?

2. Which reason from Activity 8 does she give for her opinion?
- ❑ **a.** Farmers cut down forests to make space for farming animals.
- ❑ **b.** It produces too much CO_2.
- ❑ **c.** Animals raised for meat are treated poorly.

◆ LISTEN FOR DETAILS:

10 🔊 1-45 Listen again and choose the correct answers to the questions.

1. When did Nao become a vegetarian?
- ❑ **a.** in her first year of college
- ❑ **b.** last year
- ❑ **c.** in 2018

2. What examples of nutrition did Simone mention?
- ❑ **a.** protein and energy
- ❑ **b.** protein and iron
- ❑ **c.** iron and energy

3. Which examples of vegetarian dishes did Simone give?
- ❑ **a.** soup or salads
- ❑ **b.** salads or pickles
- ❑ **c.** salads or fries

11 Work in pairs. Practice the conversation.

Simone
Nao, do you think people should eat meat?

Nao
I don't think they should. That's why I became a vegetarian last year. The main reason is that it causes environmental problems.

Asking for an example

Simone
Could you give me an example?

Giving an example in a new sentence

Nao
Sure. For instance, farmers cut down forests to make space for farming animals.

Giving an example in the middle of a sentence

Simone
I see. But isn't meat good for you? I heard it has a lot of nutrition we need, including protein and iron.

Giving an example in a new sentence

Nao
You're right that meat contains some important nutrition, but it can also be unhealthy. Let me give you an example. If people eat too much red meat, they have a higher risk of heart disease.

Giving an example in the middle of a sentence

Simone
Good point. But giving up meat isn't easy. Most restaurants serve a limited range of vegetarian dishes, such as salads or pickles.

Nao
Yeah, that's true—but there are more vegetarian restaurants these days.

DISCUSSION

12 🔊 1-46 **Find four more phrases in the conversation on page 30 to complete the chart. Then practice saying the phrases in the chart.**

💬 DISCUSSION SKILL: Supporting reasons with examples	
Asking for an example	• _____
Giving an example in a new sentence	• **For example,** farming animals produces too much CO_2. • _____, farmers cut down forests to make space for farming animals. • **One good example** is tofu burgers. • _____. If people eat too much red meat, they have a higher risk of heart disease.
Giving an example in the middle of a sentence	• Most restaurants serve a limited range of vegetarian dishes, _____ salads or pickles. • I heard it has the nutrition we need, **including** protein and iron. • There are a lot of plant-based proteins in food **like** beans and tofu.

13 **Discuss this question with your partner: *Should people eat meat?* Use the phrases in Activity 12 and the diagram below to help you.**

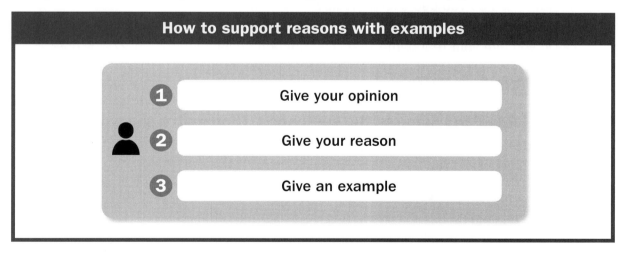

How to support reasons with examples

1 Give your opinion

2 Give your reason

3 Give an example

A: Should people eat meat?
B: Hmm. I think that …

GOAL: Learn how to continue a discussion

GET READY

1 **Discuss these questions with a partner.**

▷ How often do you use social media?
▷ Do you ever post comments to famous people's social media accounts?
▷ Do you use your real name when you post on social media? Why?/Why not?

VOCABULARY

2 🔊 **1-47** **Read and listen to the sentences. Then match the words in bold to the definitions below.**

> **1.** Children often experience **bullying** in schools, such as hitting. ___
> **2.** She made some very **cruel** comments about my dress. I was very upset. ___
> **3.** It's **impossible** to read everything on social media! ___
> **4.** The government will **pass a** new **law** next week. ___
> **5.** It's important to **prevent** children from using social media when they are young. ___
> **6.** The police should **punish** people that send horrible messages on social media. ___

a. for example, make them pay a fee or send them to prison
b. mean, not kind
c. stop something from happening
d. something that cannot be done
e. agree to introduce a new rule
f. hurting or frightening someone

LISTENING

3 🔊 1-48, 49 **Read the listening tip. Listen and repeat the example sentences.**

LISTENING TIP: Linking with s

When one word ends with *s* and the next word starts with a vowel, the words sound like they are joined. This is also true when the *s* sounds like *z*.

1. The government will pass a new law next week.
2. The police should punish people that send horrible messages on social media.

4 🔊 1-50~52 **Listen and write the missing words. Then listen and repeat the sentences.**

1. There is _____ ____ bullying on social media.
2. _____ _____ accountable for the safety of their students.
3. People make a lot of cruel _____ ____ social media.

◆ **LISTEN FOR MAIN IDEAS:**

5 🔊 1-53 **Listen to the report and choose the correct answers.**

1. According to the article, who receives negative comments on social media?
   - ❑ **a.** celebrities
   - ❑ **b.** celebrities and ordinary people
   - ❑ **c.** celebrities, ordinary people and the government

2. What did the South Korean government want to do to stop online bullying?
   - ❑ **a.** ban people from using social media
   - ❑ **b.** ban children from using social media
   - ❑ **c.** make people use their real names online

◆ **LISTEN FOR DETAILS:**

6 🔊 1-53 **Listen again and choose the correct endings to the sentences.**

1. It's often impossible to punish people that send bullying messages because they don't use their real names / they are only children.

2. The government wanted to introduce the new law so they could prevent people from / punish people for writing cruel comments.

3. The law was not passed because people were worried about losing their privacy / losing free access to social media.

Can We Stop Online Bullying?

¹_____ ___ thousands of negative comments are posted on social media every day. For example, some celebrities receive ²_____ ___ cruel comments about their appearance, their behavior, or their work.

However, ordinary people, including ³_____ _____ children, also receive bullying messages. Unfortunately, it's impossible to know who sent these cruel messages because people don't use their real names online. This means it's very hard to find and punish the people that bully others on social media.

For this reason, the South Korean government decided to introduce a new law to make people post messages using their real names. However, many ⁴_____ _____ the law. They argued that making people post messages with their real names would prevent free speech and put people's privacy at risk. After much debate, the law was not passed.

However, more than 10 ⁵_____ _____ the law was rejected, the problem has not gone away. People are still making cruel comments on social media, and without a change in the law, it's impossible to stop them.

CONVERSATION

◆ BEFORE YOU LISTEN:

8 Rank these reasons for using real names online from weakest (1) to strongest (5). Then rank the reasons against using real names online.

Reasons for using real names online

a. People would not post cruel comments. _____

b. People would be polite to each other. _____

c. People would not lie or try to trick others. _____

d. People would have more professional online names. _____

e. People would be able to find their friends online more easily. _____

Reasons against using real names online

f. People may have the same names as other people. _____

g. People would not be able to criticize the government online. _____

h. People could steal your identity and try to access your bank account. _____

i. People would be at risk from stalkers. _____

j. People could not ask for help or advice without people knowing their real names. _____

◆ LISTEN FOR MAIN IDEAS:

9 🔊 1-54 **Listen to a conversation between Sayaka and Leon. Answer the questions.**

1. Does Leon think that people should use their real names online?

2. Which reason from Activity 8 does he give for his opinion?

◆ LISTEN FOR DETAILS:

10 🔊 1-54 **Listen again. What is Leon worried about?**

❏ **a.** people finding out where he lives

❏ **b.** people stealing his money

❏ **c.** people hacking his social media account

11 Work in pairs. Practice the conversation.

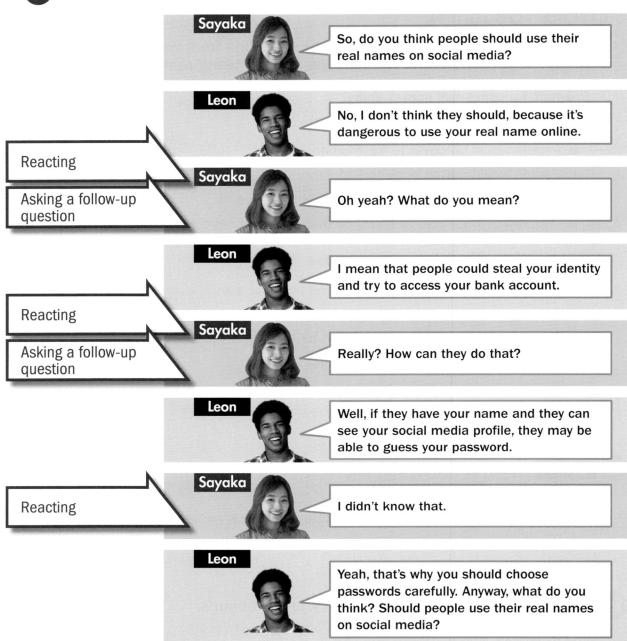

Sayaka: So, do you think people should use their real names on social media?

Leon: No, I don't think they should, because it's dangerous to use your real name online.

Reacting

Asking a follow-up question

Sayaka: Oh yeah? What do you mean?

Leon: I mean that people could steal your identity and try to access your bank account.

Reacting

Asking a follow-up question

Sayaka: Really? How can they do that?

Leon: Well, if they have your name and they can see your social media profile, they may be able to guess your password.

Reacting

Sayaka: I didn't know that.

Leon: Yeah, that's why you should choose passwords carefully. Anyway, what do you think? Should people use their real names on social media?

DISCUSSION

12 🔊 1-55 Look at the chart and then underline the reactions and follow-up questions Sayaka uses in the conversation on page 36. Then practice saying the phrases in the chart.

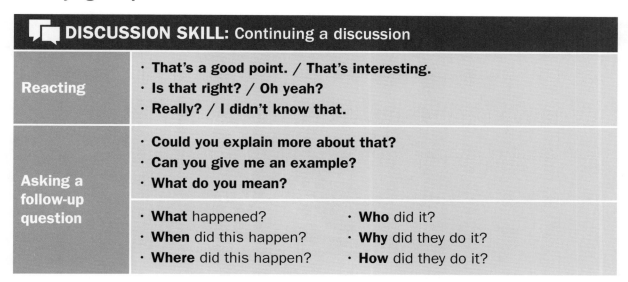

💬 DISCUSSION SKILL: Continuing a discussion	
Reacting	• That's a good point. / That's interesting. • Is that right? / Oh yeah? • Really? / I didn't know that.
Asking a follow-up question	• Could you explain more about that? • Can you give me an example? • What do you mean?
	• **What** happened? • **Who** did it? • **When** did this happen? • **Why** did they do it? • **Where** did this happen? • **How** did they do it?

13 Discuss this question with your partner: *Should the Japanese government require people to use their real names on social media?* Use the phrases in Activity 12 and the diagram below to help you.

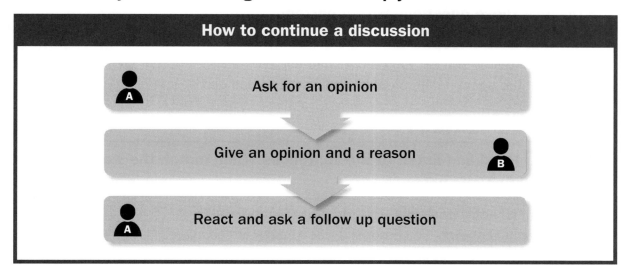

How to continue a discussion

A — Ask for an opinion

B — Give an opinion and a reason

A — React and ask a follow up question

A: Should the Japanese government require people to use their real names on social media?

B: I strongly believe that ...

Unit 7
The Soda Tax

GET READY

1 **Discuss these questions with a partner.**

▷ What kinds of foods or drinks are unhealthy?
▷ How often do you eat food that is bad for you?
▷ What are some health problems caused by a bad diet?

VOCABULARY

2 🔊 1-56 **Read and listen to the sentences. Then match the words in bold to the definitions below.**

> **1.** Young people **consume** a lot of fast food. ___
> **2.** He has **diabetes**, so he doesn't eat candies or chocolate. ___
> **3.** Doctors see a lot of people whose **diet** has made them sick. ___
> **4.** In some countries, **healthcare** is provided by the government. ___
> **5.** Many people blame fast food for the rise in **obesity**. ___
> **6.** I was surprised about how much **tax** I had to pay. ___

a. services provided to help sick people
b. a disease in which people cannot control blood sugar levels
c. being very overweight and at risk of health issues
d. eat or drink something
e. the types of food someone usually eats
f. money paid to the government

LISTENING

3 🔊 1-57, 58 **Read the listening tip. Listen and repeat the example sentences.**

LISTENING TIP: Silent letters

Some English words have silent letters. These are letters that we can see in the spelling of the word, but we do not hear when someone says the word.

1. He has diabetes so he doesn't eat candies or **chocolate**.
2. I was **surprised** about how much tax I had to pay.

4 🔊 1-59~66 **Listen and identify the letters that are not pronounced in these words. Then listen and repeat the words.**

1. business
2. cupboard
3. different
4. every

5. interesting
6. several
7. vegetable
8. island

◆ LISTEN FOR MAIN IDEAS:

5 🔊 1-67 **Listen to the report and choose the correct explanation of the soda tax.**

❏ **a.** It's a tax that manufacturers must pay.
❏ **b.** It's a tax that shops must pay.
❏ **c.** It's a tax that customers must pay.

◆ LISTEN FOR DETAILS:

6 🔊 1-67 **Listen again and write the missing numbers.**

1. The price of soda has risen by _____ % due to the soda tax.
2. Mexicans were drinking more than ___ times the recommended amount of sugar.
3. Consumption of sugary drinks fell by _____ % in 2015.
4. Experts believe that over _____ lives have been saved by the soda tax.

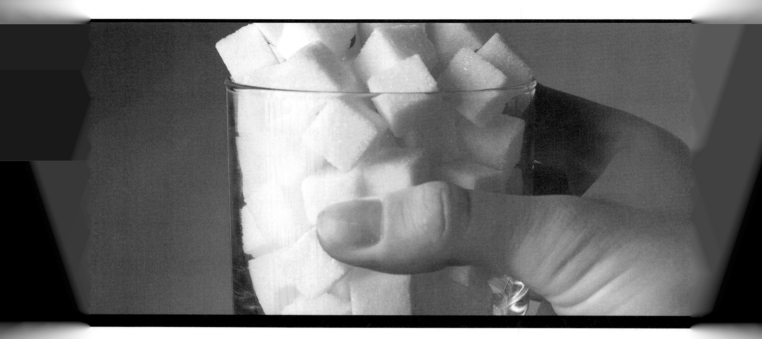

The Soda Tax

In 2014, Mexico became the first country in the world to introduce a 10% "soda tax" on sugary drinks. The idea was that higher prices [1]_____ cause people to buy fewer soft drinks and therefore consume less sugar.

According to the Coca-Cola Company, the average Mexican drank two glasses of Coca-Cola per day in 2013, which means they consumed 74 grams of sugar [2]_____ day—more than three times the amount recommended by the World Health Organization.

Having too much sugar in your diet can cause [3]_____ health problems, including diabetes, obesity, and heart problems. Treating large numbers of people with these problems increases healthcare costs, so the government hoped that the new tax would reduce the number of cases.

So, has the soda tax made a [4]_____? Well, the Mexican government announced a 5.5% drop in consumption of sugary drinks in 2014 and a further drop of 9.7% in 2015. As a result, health experts believe that over 20,000 lives have been saved.

CONVERSATION

◆ **BEFORE YOU LISTEN:**

8 Check (✓) the sentences if you agree with them. Then compare your answers with your partner. Explain your reasons.

❏ **1.** It's the government's responsibility to make sure people are healthy.

❏ **2.** Companies should not be allowed to sell very unhealthy food or drink.

❏ **3.** People who get sick due to a bad diet should pay for their healthcare.

❏ **4.** Healthcare should be paid for by the government.

❏ **5.** People will stop buying unhealthy food if it's more expensive.

❏ **6.** Companies need better labels to warn people if food or drink is unhealthy.

❏ **7.** People need to be educated about healthy eating.

❏ **8.** It's not fair to tax everyone because some people drink too much soda.

❏ **9.** People should be free to choose if they want to be healthy or unhealthy.

❏ **10.** It's not fair to tax things that people enjoy eating and drinking.

◆ **LISTEN FOR MAIN IDEAS:**

9 🔊 1-68 Listen to Junichi and Isobel discussing the soda tax. Do they think it's a good idea?

1. Isobel's opinion: good idea / not sure / bad idea

2. Junichi's opinion: good idea / not sure / bad idea

◆ **LISTEN FOR DETAILS:**

10 🔊 1-68 Listen again and choose the correct words to complete the sentences.

1. Isobel thinks that most people <u>drink</u> / <u>don't drink</u> a lot of soda.

2. Isobel thinks that most people that drink soda <u>are</u> / <u>aren't</u> rich.

3. Junichi thinks that people <u>read</u> / <u>don't read</u> health warnings on food labels.

11 Work in pairs. Practice the conversation.

Junichi: That was an interesting report, wasn't it? Do you think that all countries should have a soda tax?

Explaining in more detail

Isobel: Hmm. I don't think it's a good idea because it's not fair for most people. What I mean is that most people don't drink a lot of soda every day, so they shouldn't have to pay more for it because other people drink too much.

Junichi: Yeah, I suppose that's true.

Adding another reason

Isobel: And on top of that, I'm sure that most people that drink soda, such as teenagers and students, don't have much money. Is it fair to take more money from them?

Providing more specific details

Junichi: That's a good point, but I think a soda tax is a good idea because it's the most effective way to discourage people from consuming too much sugar. In fact, I don't think that most people read health warnings on product labels. They will notice a price increase, though.

Isobel: You may be right, but I still think they're taxing the wrong people. Shouldn't they tax the companies that make these unhealthy products?

DISCUSSION

12 🔊 1-69 **Look at the chart. Underline the phrases in the conversation on page 42 that Junichi and Isobel use to expand their answers. Then practice saying the phrases in the chart.**

💬 DISCUSSION SKILL: Expanding your answer	
Explaining in more detail	· **Let me elaborate**. Most people don't drink a lot of soda, so ... · **I mean**, some people don't drink a lot of soda, so ... · **What I mean is that** some people don't drink a lot of soda, so ...
Providing more specific details	· **In fact,** I don't think people read health warnings. · **Actually,** I don't think people read health warnings. · **As a matter of fact,** I don't think people read health warnings.
Adding another reason	· **Also,** most people that drink soda don't have much money. · **On top of that**, most people that drink soda don't have much money. · **Another reason is that** most people that drink soda don't have much money.

13 **Discuss this question with your partner:** *Should Japan introduce a soda tax?* **Use the phrases in Activity 12 and the diagram below to help you.**

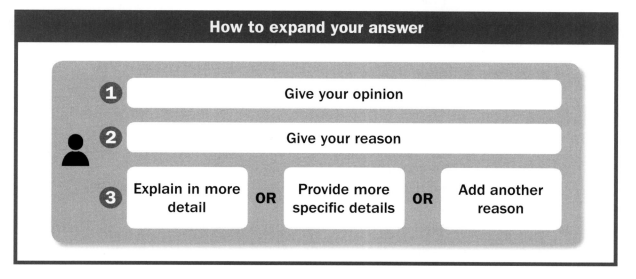

How to expand your answer

1 Give your opinion

2 Give your reason

3 Explain in more detail OR Provide more specific details OR Add another reason

A: I read that Mexico introduced a soda tax. Do you think Japan should introduce one too?
B: I strongly believe that ...

Unit 8

Overtourism

GET READY

1 **Discuss these questions with a partner.**

▷ What are some of the most popular destinations for tourists in Japan?
▷ Why does the Japanese government want more tourists to visit Japan?
▷ What are some problems caused by tourists?

VOCABULARY

2 🔊 1-70 **Read and listen to the sentences. Then match the words in bold to the definitions below.**

> **1.** There is a lot of **construction** in the city right now. ___
> **2.** It's a popular **destination** for tourists because of its culture and history. ___
> **3.** It's a beautiful place, so **it's no surprise that** tourists love it. ___
> **4.** The mayor promised to improve people's **quality of life**. ___
> **5.** We should **set a limit** on the number of visitors to stop it from becoming crowded. ___
> **6.** The city **suffers from** overcrowding in the tourist season. ___

a. happiness and comfort
b. building work
c. decide a maximum
d. place you travel to
e. experiences something negative
f. it's obvious that

LISTENING

3 🔊 1-71~73 **Read the listening tip. Listen and repeat the example sentences.**

LISTENING TIP: Weak forms of *and*, *of*, and *to*

Some words have strong and weak forms. We usually say the weak forms.

1. **and:** It's a popular destination for tourists because of its culture **and** history.
2. **of:** There is a lot **of** construction in the city right now.
3. **to:** We should set a limit on the number of visitors **to** stop it from becoming crowded.

4 🔊 1-74~76 **Listen and write the missing words. Then listen and repeat the sentences.**

1. Some tourists don't know that it's not polite ____ _____ loudly on the train.
2. We went to the museum _____ _____ _____ square this morning.
3. There are a lot ____ _____ at the beach, so let's go somewhere else.

◆ **LISTEN FOR MAIN IDEAS:**

5 🔊 1-77 **Listen to the report and choose the best summary.**

❑ **a.** Barcelona doesn't suffer from overtourism yet, but it is likely to soon.
❑ **b.** Barcelona is very popular, so it suffers from overtourism.
❑ **c.** Barcelona used to suffer from overtourism, but the mayor solved the problem.

◆ **LISTEN FOR DETAILS:**

6 🔊 1-77 **Listen again and choose the correct answers.**

1. According to the speaker, why is Barcelona a popular tourist destination?
   ❑ **a.** Because it has a good location, beautiful buildings, and delicious food.
   ❑ **b.** Because it has a beautiful beach, amazing museums, and fun things to do.
   ❑ **c.** Because it has fantastic weather, fantastic shopping, and great restaurants.

2. How many visitors stayed in Barcelona in 2019?
   ❑ **a.** 1.6 million
   ❑ **b.** 1.7 million
   ❑ **c.** 9.5 million

3. What action did the mayor take to stop overtourism?
   ❑ **a.** She set a limit on the number of visitors.
   ❑ **b.** She set a limit on the number of beds for tourists.
   ❑ **c.** She set a limit on the number of tour groups.

The Challenge of Overtourism

Barcelona is a beautiful city near the sea with amazing buildings and wonderful food—so it's no surprise that it's ¹_____ ____ the most popular tourist destinations in Europe.

However, in recent years, the ²_____ ____ visitors has increased dramatically. In 1990, there were 1.7 million overnight visitors; in 2019, there were 9.5 million. And for a small city—Barcelona has a population of 1.6 million—that is a lot of guests ³___ _____ after.

As a result of the increase in tourism, the streets are crowded, the price ⁴___ _____ has gone up, and pollution has increased. In short, Barcelona is suffering from overtourism, and this is affecting the quality of life of the people that live there.

To try to solve the problem, the mayor of Barcelona has banned the construction of new hotels ⁵_____ ____ a limit on the number of beds available ⁶___ _____. However, this may not be enough to stop the effects of overtourism.

CONVERSATION

◆ **BEFORE YOU LISTEN:**

8 **Look at this list of ideas for solving the problems of overtourism in Kyoto. In pairs, score each one from 0 (terrible idea) to 5 (fantastic idea).**

_____ 1. build a new public transportation system that can handle more people

_____ 2. close the city to tourists for part of the year

_____ 3. charge higher prices to discourage people from visiting

_____ 4. create a Kyoto theme park in a different area and ask tourists to go there

_____ 5. limit the number of hotel rooms that are available

_____ 6. limit the number of people that can visit Kyoto at the same time

_____ 7. pay local people to move to a different city

_____ 8. promote alternative destinations to tourists

_____ 9. provide an app to show which places are busy

_____ 10. sell tickets that only allow people to visit sites at specific times

◆ **LISTEN FOR MAIN IDEAS:**

9 🔊 1-78 **Listen to Antonio and Rie talking about overtourism in Kyoto. Which ideas from Activity 8 do they discuss?**

◆ **LISTEN FOR DETAILS:**

10 🔊 1-78 **Listen again and answer the questions.**

1. What problem of overtourism does Rie mention?

   ❏ **a.** busy shops

   ❏ **b.** crowded buses

   ❏ **c.** expensive prices

2. Why does Antonio reject Rie's first idea?

   ❏ **a.** It's hard to stop people entering the city.

   ❏ **b.** Kyoto needs money from tourism.

   ❏ **c.** It would be difficult for businesspeople.

3. Where does Antonio suggest the city sell tickets to tourist sites?

   ❏ **a.** at the train station

   ❏ **b.** in shops in the city center

   ❏ **c.** at the tourist information center

⑪ Work in pairs. Practice the conversation.

Antonio: Overtourism sounds bad in Barcelona. Does Japan have overtourism, too?

Rie: Yes, especially in Kyoto. The buses are always crowded, so it's hard for local people.

Asking for a suggestion →

Antonio: So, <u>what should</u> the government <u>do about it?</u>

Making a suggestion →

Rie: That's a good question. I think they <u>ought to</u> limit the number of people that can visit Kyoto at the same time.

Rejecting a suggestion →

Antonio: <u>I'm not sure about that.</u> I think it's difficult to stop people from coming into the city.

Making a suggestion →

Rie: Um, well, <u>I suggest</u> they sell tickets that only allow people to visit the famous sites at specific times. That would reduce the number of people traveling to these places at the same time.

Accepting a suggestion →

Antonio: <u>That's a good idea.</u> They should sell these tickets at the tourist information center in the city center.

Rie: Yes, I like that idea. Do you have any other ideas?

DISCUSSION

12 🔊 1-79 Find two more phrases in the conversation on page 48 to complete the chart below. Then practice saying the phrases in the chart.

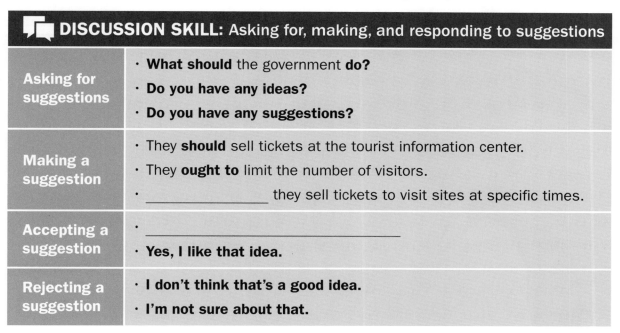

💬 DISCUSSION SKILL: Asking for, making, and responding to suggestions	
Asking for suggestions	• **What should** the government **do?** • **Do you have any ideas?** • **Do you have any suggestions?**
Making a suggestion	• They **should** sell tickets at the tourist information center. • They **ought to** limit the number of visitors. • _____ they sell tickets to visit sites at specific times.
Accepting a suggestion	• _____ • **Yes, I like that idea.**
Rejecting a suggestion	• **I don't think that's a good idea.** • **I'm not sure about that.**

13 Work in pairs. Think of suggestions to solve these problems. Use the phrases from Activity 12 and the diagram below to help you.

- Kyoto is suffering from overtourism.
- The government wants tourists to visit other parts of Japan.
- Tourists don't understand Japanese customs.

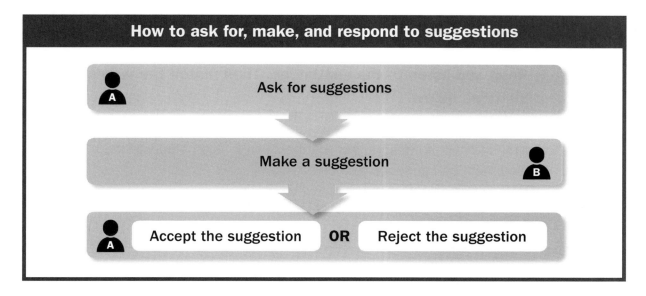

How to ask for, make, and respond to suggestions

A — Ask for suggestions

Make a suggestion — B

A — Accept the suggestion **OR** Reject the suggestion

A: Kyoto is suffering from overtourism. What should the government do?
B: I suggest that ...

Unit 9
Improving Education

GET READY

1 **Discuss these questions with a partner.**

▷ Did you like school? Why?/Why not?
▷ How much homework did you do every day?
▷ Did you like doing tests? Why?/Why not?

VOCABULARY

2 🔊 2-1 **Read and listen to the sentences. Then match the words in bold to the definitions below.**

> **1.** Today's test is **based on** the book we read—so I hope you remember it! ___
> **2.** **Experts**, such as professors, say that homework helps students learn. ___
> **3.** I studied hard, so I got good **grades** at school. ___
> **4.** Students get **stressed** when they have too much work to do. ___
> **5.** I passed the exam **whereas** Yukiko failed it. ___
> **6.** Who is **willing** to do their presentation first? ___

a. happy to do something
b. scores
c. but; in comparison
d. annoyed or worried
e. people who know a lot about something
f. using facts or ideas from something

50

LISTENING

3 🔊 2-2~4 **Read the listening tip. Listen and repeat the example sentences.**

LISTENING TIP: Weak forms of *can* and *be*

Many common words have strong and weak forms. We usually use the weak forms in conversation whereas we use strong forms to emphasize words.

1. **Weak:** Students **can** wear sneakers at school.
   Strong: Students can't wear jeans, but they **can** wear sneakers.

2. **Weak:** The exams **are** very difficult.
   Strong: The exams aren't long, but they **are** very difficult.

3. **Weak:** Our school **is** really good.
   Strong: Our school isn't very big, but it **is** really good.

4 🔊 2-5~7 **Listen and write the missing words. Then listen and repeat the sentences.**

1. Some students _____ _____ the computers.

2. That student ___ _____ the library.

3. Students _____ _____ the gym.

◆ **LISTEN FOR MAIN IDEAS:**

5 🔊 2-8 **Listen to the report and choose the reason that the speaker thinks schools in Finland are so successful.**

❑ **a.** Because the teachers are very strict.

❑ **b.** Because the students are not stressed.

❑ **c.** Because the school days are longer than in other countries.

◆ **LISTEN FOR DETAILS:**

6 🔊 2-8 **Listen again and decide if each sentence is true or false.**

1. Students in Finland start school very early.	T / F
2. Students in Finland have a rest after each class.	T / F
3. Students in Finland do a lot of homework every day.	T / F
4. Students in Finland do not have exams.	T / F
5. Teachers can choose what to teach their students.	T / F

The Best Schools in the World

Which country has the best schools in the world? According to several experts, the answer is Finland. So, what makes its education system so special?

One difference is that schools ¹_____ more relaxed. Lessons don't start until after 9:00—sometimes not until 9:45—and students ²_____ take long breaks between classes. This means that students ³_____ well rested and ready to learn.

Also, there ⁴___ very little homework. Whereas students in other countries do several hours of homework every night, in Finland students only do about 30 minutes.

Another big difference ⁵___ that there are no tests. Teachers decide students' grades based on their classwork.

Teachers also have more freedom to decide what to teach, so they ⁶_____ choose the material to suit their students' interests and needs.

All together, these differences mean that students ⁷_____ less tired, less stressed, and more willing to learn. Will other countries take the same approach?

CONVERSATION

◆ **BEFORE YOU LISTEN:**

8 Complete the arguments for and against taking exams with the words in the boxes.

Arguments for taking exams

achievement · check · compare · keep · skills

1. Exams motivate students to _____ studying.
2. Studying for exams builds time management _____.
3. Passing an exam gives students a feeling of _____.
4. Exams are a good way to _____ if someone has learned something.
5. Exams are a good way to _____ students from different schools.

Arguments against taking exams

cause · cramming · memory · time · without

6. Exams are stressful and can _____ health problems.
7. Exams test _____ rather than understanding.
8. Teachers waste _____ teaching students about the exam format.
9. Students can pass exams _____ doing any work in class.
10. Exams encourage _____, which doesn't lead to long-term remembering.

◆ **LISTEN FOR MAIN IDEAS:**

9 🔊 2-9 **Listen to a conversation between Monika and Keisuke. Answer the questions.**

1. Does Keisuke think Japanese schools should stop using exams?
2. How many reasons does he give?

◆ **LISTEN FOR DETAILS:**

10 🔊 2-9 **Listen again. Which reasons from Activity 8 does Keisuke give for his opinion?**

11 Work in pairs. Practice the conversation.

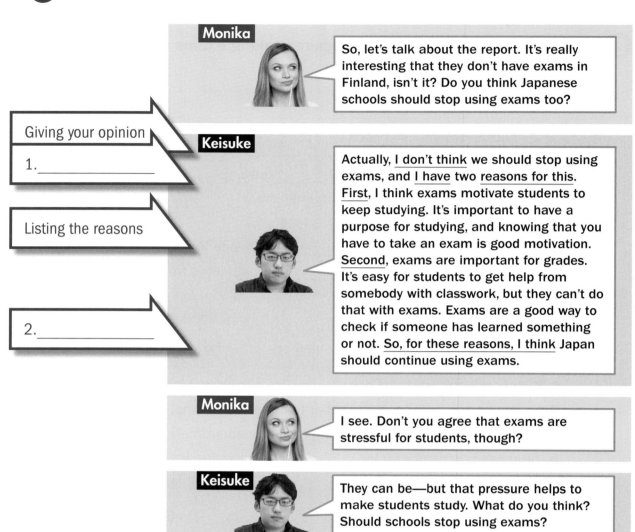

Monika

So, let's talk about the report. It's really interesting that they don't have exams in Finland, isn't it? Do you think Japanese schools should stop using exams too?

Giving your opinion

1. _____

Listing the reasons

2. _____

Keisuke

Actually, I don't think we should stop using exams, and I have two reasons for this. First, I think exams motivate students to keep studying. It's important to have a purpose for studying, and knowing that you have to take an exam is good motivation. Second, exams are important for grades. It's easy for students to get help from somebody with classwork, but they can't do that with exams. Exams are a good way to check if someone has learned something or not. So, for these reasons, I think Japan should continue using exams.

Monika

I see. Don't you agree that exams are stressful for students, though?

Keisuke

They can be—but that pressure helps to make students study. What do you think? Should schools stop using exams?

DISCUSSION

12 🔊 2-10 **Look at the chart. Add labels to the conversation on page 54. Then practice saying the phrases in the chart.**

💬 DISCUSSION SKILL: Supporting your opinion with multiple reasons	
Giving your opinion	· **I strongly believe that** we should stop using exams. · **I think** we should stop using exams. · **I'm not sure, but perhaps** we shouldn't stop using exams.
Explaining that you have multiple reasons	· **I have** two **reasons for this**. · **There are** three **reasons for this**.
Listing the reasons	· **First**, exams motivate students to study. **Second**, exams are important for grades. **Finally**, exams help people learn. · **One reason is** exams are stressful. **Another reason** is exams take a lot of time.
Repeating your opinion	· **So, for these reasons, I think** Japan should stop using exams. · **So that's why I believe** Japan should continue using exams.

13 **Discuss this question with your partner: *Should Japanese schools stop using exams?* Use the phrases in Activity 12 and the diagram below to help you.**

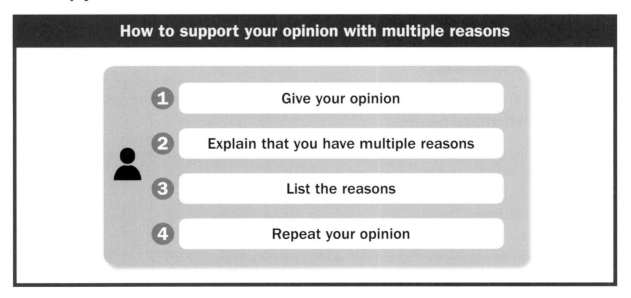

How to support your opinion with multiple reasons

1. Give your opinion
2. Explain that you have multiple reasons
3. List the reasons
4. Repeat your opinion

A: Should Japanese schools stop using exams?
B: I'm not sure, but perhaps ...

Unit 10
Voting Age

GOAL: Learn how to check your understanding

GET READY

1 **Discuss these questions with a partner.**

▷ Have you ever voted?
▷ Did you learn about voting in school?
▷ Are you interested in politics? Why?/Why not?

VOCABULARY

2 🔊 2-11 **Read and listen to the sentences. Then match the words in bold to the definitions below.**

> **1.** In most countries, people reach **adulthood** when they are 18. ___
> **2.** This year I can vote in my first **election**! ___
> **3.** Most 18-year-olds are **mature** enough to make important decisions. ___
> **4.** The **minimum** age for drinking alcohol varies from country to country. ___
> **5.** Politicians tend to make **policies** that appeal to older people. ___
> **6.** There are many **political parties** in Japan, such as the LDP. ___

a. the period of life when you are physically and mentally developed
b. groups of politicians with similar ideas
c. a process in which people choose leaders
d. lowest or smallest
e. ideas or proposals
f. mentally and emotionally developed

56

LISTENING

3 🔊 2-12, 13 **Read the listening tip. Listen and repeat the example sentences.**

LISTENING TIP: Linking with vowels

When one word ends with a vowel sound and the next word begins with a vowel sound, we link the words with a *y* or *w* sound.

1. **When the first word ends with an *a*, *e* or *i* sound, we link with a *y* sound.**
   · In most countries, people reach adulthood when th<u>ey a</u>re 18.
2. **When the first word ends with an *o* or *u* sound, we link with a *w* sound.**
   · Politicians tend to make policies that appeal t<u>o o</u>lder people.

4 🔊 2-14~17 **Listen and write the missing words. Then listen and repeat the sentences.**

1. _____ ___ graduating from university next month.
2. I often ____ _____ with my classmates after lectures.
3. _____ _____ the most mature students in my class.
4. Students can learn about voting _____ _____ research.

◆ **LISTEN FOR MAIN IDEAS:**

5 🔊 2-18 **Listen to the report and choose the best summary.**

❑ **a.** Most countries want to raise the voting age.

❑ **b.** The speaker believes that 16-year-olds should not be able to vote.

❑ **c.** There are reasons for and against allowing 16-year-olds to vote.

◆ **LISTEN FOR DETAILS:**

6 🔊 2-18 **Listen again and complete the sentences.**

1. The main reason for lowering the age was to make people <u>more interested in politics</u> / <u>more likely to vote in adulthood</u>.
2. Research shows that people who can vote from the age of 16 are <u>more</u> / <u>less</u> likely to vote in adulthood.
3. The speaker believes that changing the voting age will also change <u>the age of politicians</u> / <u>the policies made by political parties</u>.

What should the voting age be?

It is now more than 10 years since Austria became the first country in Europe
¹_____ _____ 16-year-olds to vote in all elections—local, state and national.

The main reason for lowering ²_____ _____ was to make young people
more interested in politics. And it seems to be working. The results in Austria
suggest that if students learn about their country's political system in high
school, and begin voting at 16, ³_____ _____ more likely to continue voting
in adulthood. Also, if young people can vote, political parties will be more
likely to create policies that appeal to younger people rather than just middle-
aged and older people.

For these reasons, several countries already have a voting age of 16,
including Brazil and Argentina, and it's being considered in others, such as
Australia, ⁴_____ _____, and ⁵_____ _____. Not everybody agrees, of course.
Some people argue that 16-year-olds are not yet mature enough to make such
important decisions—and ⁶_____ _____ suggest raising the minimum age to
as high as 25!

CONVERSATION

◆ **BEFORE YOU LISTEN:**

8 Look at these sentences. Which ones are reasons for allowing 16-year-olds to vote, and which ones are against allowing 16-year-olds to vote?

	for	against
1. They are not mature enough to make important decisions.		
2. Students are too busy studying to think about politics.		
3. It's very expensive for the country to deal with a lot of extra voters.		
4. They will be more likely to vote as adults if they start young.		
5. Voting in elections makes people care more about society.		
6. Political parties will make policies for both young and old people.		
7. Some teenagers are very mature for their age.		
8. You need a lot of life experience to understand politics.		

◆ **LISTEN FOR MAIN IDEAS:**

9 🔊 2-19 Listen to a conversation between Takuya and Chanda. Answer the questions.

1. Does Chanda think 16-year-olds should be allowed to vote?

2. Which of the reasons from Activity 8 does she give for her opinion?

◆ **LISTEN FOR DETAILS:**

10 🔊 2-19 Listen again. Decide if each sentence is true or false.

1. Chanda thinks voting gives people a chance to learn about social issues.   T / F

2. Takuya thinks that all teenagers should be able to vote.   T / F

11 Work in pairs. Practice the conversation.

Takuya: Chanda, I read that some countries, such as Austria, have lowered the voting age. What do you think? Should 16-year-olds be allowed to vote?

Chanda: Yes, they should. Voting in elections makes people care more about society.

1. _____

Takuya: Can I check my understanding? You mean that voting gives people a chance to think and learn more about social issues?

2. _____

Chanda: Exactly. What about you?

Takuya: I think so too! Adding to what you said, I think teenagers should be able to vote because some of them are very mature for their age.

3. _____

Chanda: So you think that *all* teenagers should be able to vote?

4. _____

Takuya: Not exactly. I mean that 16-year-olds already make decisions about study and part-time jobs, so I think they are old enough to think about voting too.

5. _____

Chanda: Okay. I got it.

DISCUSSION

12 🔊 2-20 **Look at the chart. Add labels to the conversation on page 60. Then practice saying the phrases in the chart.**

💬 DISCUSSION SKILL: Checking your understanding

Checking understanding	• **Can I check my understanding?**
	   • **Did you say that** students are too busy to think about politics?
	   • **You mean that** voting helps people think about social issues?
	   • **So you think that** all teenagers should be able to vote?
	 • **Is that correct?**

Confirming the meaning	• **Yes, that's right.** • **Exactly.**
Clarifying the meaning	• **Not exactly. I mean that** 16-year-olds already make decisions. • **Actually, I meant** some 16-year-olds are already mature.
Confirming understanding	• **I see.** • **Okay. I got it.**

13 **Discuss this question with your partner:** *What age should people be allowed to do the things below?* **Use the phrases in Activity 12 and the diagram below to help you.**

> vote / get married / drink alcohol / get a driver's license / smoke / get a credit card

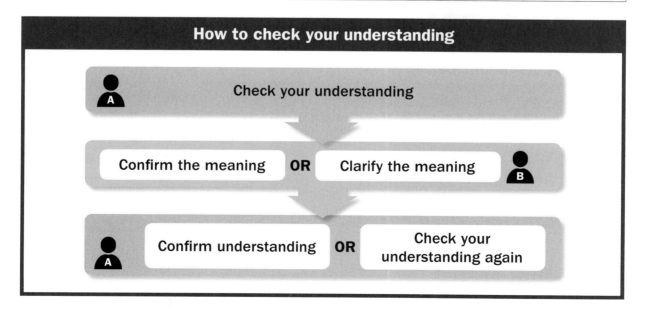

How to check your understanding

A — Check your understanding
↓
Confirm the meaning **OR** Clarify the meaning — B
↓
A — Confirm understanding **OR** Check your understanding again

A: What age should people be allowed to vote?
B: Hmm. Well, I think ...

Unit 11
Rethinking Zoos

GOAL: Learn how to lead a discussion

GET READY

1 **Discuss these questions with a partner.**

▷ How often do you visit zoos or aquariums?
▷ Do you like zoos or aquariums? Why?/Why not?
▷ Do you think zoos are good for animals? Why?/Why not?

VOCABULARY

2 🔊 2-21 **Read and listen to the sentences. Then match the words in bold to the definitions below.**

1. Because of **breeding** programs, there are now a lot of pandas in zoos. ___
2. There have been many local **conservation** projects to protect lakes and parks. ___
3. Zoo **enclosures** should match the conditions in which animals live in the wild. ___
4. Pandas were **endangered**, but now their numbers are increasing. ___
5. She was **praised** by animal welfare groups for her work to protect animals. ___
6. If we are not careful, human behavior may cause some **species** to die out, such as tigers and Asian elephants. ___

a. groups of animals or plants that are similar to each other
b. helping animals to have babies
c. protection of plants and animals from human activity
d. said positive things about someone or something
e. areas surrounded by fences or other barriers
f. at risk of dying out

LISTENING

3 🔊 2-22, 23 **Read the listening tip. Listen and repeat the example sentences.**

LISTENING TIP: Linking with _t_

When one word ends with _t_ and the next word starts with a vowel, the words often sound like they are joined. The _t_ sound sometimes becomes a _d_ sound.

1. Because of breeding programs, there are now a lot of pandas in zoos.
2. She was praised by animal welfare groups for her work to protect animals.

4 🔊 2-24~27 **Listen and write the missing words. Then listen and repeat the sentences.**

1. If you go outside, you should _____ ____ a sweater.

2. I think we need to _____ _____ from humans.

3. The _____ _____ is for animals to live in their natural environment.

4. When I was in elementary school, we _____ __ hamster in our classroom.

◆ **LISTEN FOR MAIN IDEAS:**

5 🔊 2-28 **Listen to the report and choose the best summary.**

❑ **a.** Costa Rica decided to ban zoos for the benefit of animals.

❑ **b.** Costa Rica decided to ban zoos for the benefit of people.

❑ **c.** Costa Rica decided to ban zoos for the benefit of people and animals.

◆ **LISTEN FOR DETAILS:**

6 🔊 2-28 **Listen again and choose the correct answers.**

1. Why did animal welfare supporters praise Costa Rica's decision?

❑ **a.** Because polar bear enclosures are too small and warm.

❑ **b.** Because they think animal enclosures cause the animals stress.

❑ **c.** Because zoos are not as popular as they used to be.

2. Why do some animal lovers support zoos?

❑ **a.** Because zoos with breeding campaigns help to protect endangered animals.

❑ **b.** Because zoos teach us more about animals than nature documentaries.

❑ **c.** Because zoos keep rare animals, such as pandas.

3. What does the report say about the future of zoos?

❑ **a.** Zoos and aquariums are likely to disappear in the near future.

❑ **b.** Zoos and aquariums are unlikely to disappear in the near future.

❑ **c.** Zoos are likely to disappear in the near future but aquariums will not.

A Ban on Zoos?

In 2009, the small Central American nation of Costa Rica made international news when ¹__ _____ a plan to close all zoos in the country. Although this has yet to happen, the announcement has led to a ²_____ _____ the role of zoos and aquariums in society.

Animal welfare supporters praised Costa Rica for the plan. They argue that zoo animals are often ³_____ ___ small or unsuitable spaces that cause them physical and mental stress. A typical polar bear enclosure, for instance, is much smaller and warmer than the animal's natural living conditions.

Of course, many animal lovers support the existence of zoos. Some say that they are important for conservation because breeding programs help to ⁴_____ _____ species. Others argue that zoos play a vital role in educating and inspiring children.

Despite these differing opinions, zoos and aquariums remain incredibly popular. And with more than 700 million visitors worldwide each year, it seems they are not going to disappear soon.

CONVERSATION

◆ BEFORE YOU LISTEN:

8 Rank these reasons for banning zoos from weakest (1) to strongest (5). Then rank the reasons against banning zoos.

Reasons for banning zoos

a. Zoo enclosures cause animals physical and emotional stress. _____

b. Animals should be free to live in the wild. _____

c. Zoos prioritize the entertainment of people over the welfare of animals. _____

d. Only a few zoos have breeding programs—they aren't so important for conservation. _____

e. We can learn more about animals from nature documentaries. _____

Reasons against banning zoos

f. People love looking at animals. _____

g. People can learn a lot about animals from visiting zoos. _____

h. Zoos and aquariums are extremely popular. _____

i. Zoos can inspire children to work for animal welfare in the future. _____

j. Breeding animals in zoos can help to save endangered animals. _____

◆ LISTEN FOR MAIN IDEAS:

9 🔊 2-29 **Listen to a conversation between Sara, Jess, Shota and Bong. Sara is leading the discussion. Answer the questions.**

1. Does Jess think zoos should be banned?

2. Which of the reasons from Activity 8 does she give for her answer?

◆ LISTEN FOR DETAILS:

10 🔊 2-29 **Listen again. What other reason does Shota give for banning zoos?**

❑ **a.** Zoos are for the entertainment of people, not the welfare of animals.

❑ **b.** Only a few zoos have breeding programs—they aren't so important for conservation.

❑ **c.** We can learn more about animals from nature documentaries than zoos.

11 **Work in groups of four. Practice the conversation.**

Introducing the topic

Introducing the first question

Sara 
Today's topic is animals. We have four questions to discuss. Let's start with the first question. Should we ban zoos? What do you think, Jess?

Jess
I think we should. The main reason is that animals should be free to live in the wild. On top of that, zoo enclosures cause animals physical and emotional stress.

Involving people

Sara 
Interesting. Shota, do you agree with Jess?

Shota 
Yes, I do. In addition, zoos are not really necessary. What I mean is, we can learn more about animals from nature documentaries than zoos.

Bong 
That's a good point, but zoos and aquariums are extremely popular.

Shota 
That's true.

Checking everyone has finished the question

Sara 
Does anyone have anything to add?

Bong
Jess
Shota 
No.

Moving to a new question

Sara 
Okay, let's move on to the next question ...

DISCUSSION

12 🔊 2-30 **Look at the chart. Check (✓) the phrases that Sara uses in the conversation on page 66. Then practice saying the phrases in the chart.**

💬 DISCUSSION SKILL: Leading a discussion	
Introducing the topic	• **Today's topic is** animals. • **Today we're going to discuss** zoos.
Introducing the first question	• **Let's start with the first question.** Should we ban zoos?
Involving people	• **What do you think**, Jess? • **Do you agree with** Jess? • **Does everyone agree?**
Checking everyone has finished the question	• **Does anyone have anything to add?**
Moving to a new question	• **Let's move on to the next question.**
Ending the discussion	• **Thanks everyone. That was a good discussion.**

13 **Discuss these questions with your partner or group. Take turns leading the discussion. Use the phrases in Activity 12 and the diagram below to help you.**

- Should zoos be banned?
- Is it okay to keep pets in small apartments?
- Are pet cafes good for animals?
- Which are better as pets, cats or dogs?

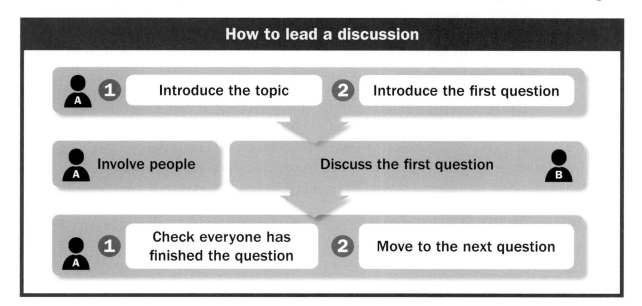

How to lead a discussion

A **1** Introduce the topic   **2** Introduce the first question

A Involve people   Discuss the first question **B**

A **1** Check everyone has finished the question   **2** Move to the next question

A: Today's topic is animals. Let's start with the first question. Should zoos be banned?

Alternative Energy

GOAL: Learn how to discuss the pros and cons of something

GET READY

1 **Discuss these questions with a partner.**

▷ What are some sources of alternative energy?
▷ Why do some people think countries should use more alternative energy?
▷ Where does Japan get its electricity from?

VOCABULARY

2 🔊 2-31 **Read and listen to the sentences. Then match the words in bold to the definitions below.**

1. Many farmers have started producing **biomass** to sell to energy companies. ___
2. Burning **fossil fuels** has such a bad impact on the environment. ___
3. Japan uses nuclear power to **generate** some of its electricity. ___
4. Countries can use rivers or the sea to create **hydroelectric power**. ___
5. Countries should switch over from coal and gas to **renewable sources of energy**. ___
6. The largest wind farm in Japan has 40 **wind turbines**. ___

a. coal, oil, and gas
b. energy created using water
c. plant and animal waste that is burned to create energy
d. produce or create (energy)
e. machines that make energy from wind
f. the sun, wind, water, etc.

LISTENING

3 🔊 2-32, 33 **Read the listening tip. Listen and repeat the example sentences.**

LISTENING TIP: Linking with *ch*

Words that end in a *ch* sound often link with words that start with a vowel.

1. Burning fossil fuels has such a bad impact on the environment.
2. Countries should switch over from coal and gas to renewable sources of energy.

4 🔊 2-34~36 **Listen and write the missing words. Then listen and repeat the sentences.**

1. Wind turbines, _____ _____ often 100 meters tall, can ruin a nice view.
2. There are various types of alternative energy and _____ ____ them has good points and bad points.
3. We need to _____ _____ children about climate change.

◆ **LISTEN FOR MAIN IDEAS:**

5 🔊 2-37 **Listen to the report and choose the best summary.**

❑ **a.** Brazil uses more alternative energy than most other countries.
❑ **b.** Brazil uses a similar amount of alternative energy to most other countries.
❑ **c.** Brazil uses less alternative energy than most other countries.

◆ **LISTEN FOR DETAILS:**

6 🔊 2-37 **Listen again and choose the correct answers to the questions.**

1. What percentage of Brazil's electricity comes from renewable sources of energy?
❑ **a.** 25%
❑ **b.** 80%
❑ **c.** 100%

2. Which source provides the most electricity for Brazil?
❑ **a.** fossil fuels
❑ **b.** hydroelectric power
❑ **c.** solar power

3. According to the speaker, what is likely to happen in the near future?
❑ **a.** All countries will only use alternative energy.
❑ **b.** Brazil will start to use biomass.
❑ **c.** Brazil will get all its energy from renewable sources.

An Alternative Approach

As the world tries to prevent climate change, countries have promised to get as [1]_____ _____ as possible from renewable sources. However, most of them still rely on fossil fuels. In fact, only 25% of the world's electricity comes from alternative energy.

One country has made more progress than others, though: Brazil generates more than 80% of its electricity from alternative energy. This is because Brazil is [2]_____ ___ natural resources.

It has a long coastline and several large rivers, [3]_____ _____ it to generate most of its electricity from hydroelectric power. The climate is also perfect for using alternative energy. Some areas have very strong winds so they can use wind turbines, and it is [4]_____ ___ sunny place that they can use solar power too. Finally, there is a lot of good land for farming, so many people grow crops [5]_____ _____ used as biomass.

This combined approach is working so well that Brazil is confident that it can get 100% of its electricity from renewable sources in the near future. Let's hope that more countries can [6]_____ ___ .

CONVERSATION

◆ **BEFORE YOU LISTEN:**

8 Match these sentences to the energy sources below. Some sentences match to more than one energy source.

a. It can be used in many locations.

b. It costs a lot to build.

c. It harms wildlife.

d. It can be damaged by the weather

e. It's very noisy.

f. It's not reliable all year.

g. It provides jobs for people.

h. It needs a lot of land.

i. It spoils the view.

j. It stops things from being wasted.

k. It doesn't produce harmful gases.

l. It produces CO_2.

m. It can store drinking water.

n. It doesn't produce waste.

	Advantages	Disadvantages
Solar power	a,	
Wind power		
Hydroelectric power		
Biomass		

◆ **LISTEN FOR MAIN IDEAS:**

9 🔊 2-38 Listen to a conversation between Richard, Wakako, and Pedro. Which type of energy are they talking about?

❑ **a.** biomass

❑ **b.** fossil fuels

❑ **c.** solar power

❑ **d.** wind power

◆ **LISTEN FOR DETAILS:**

10 🔊 2-38 Listen again and complete the notes.

Advantages of this kind of fuel

1. It uses up _____.

2. It's _____.

Disadvantages of this kind of fuel

1. It needs a lot of _____.

2. It produces _____.

11 Work in groups of three. Practice the conversation.

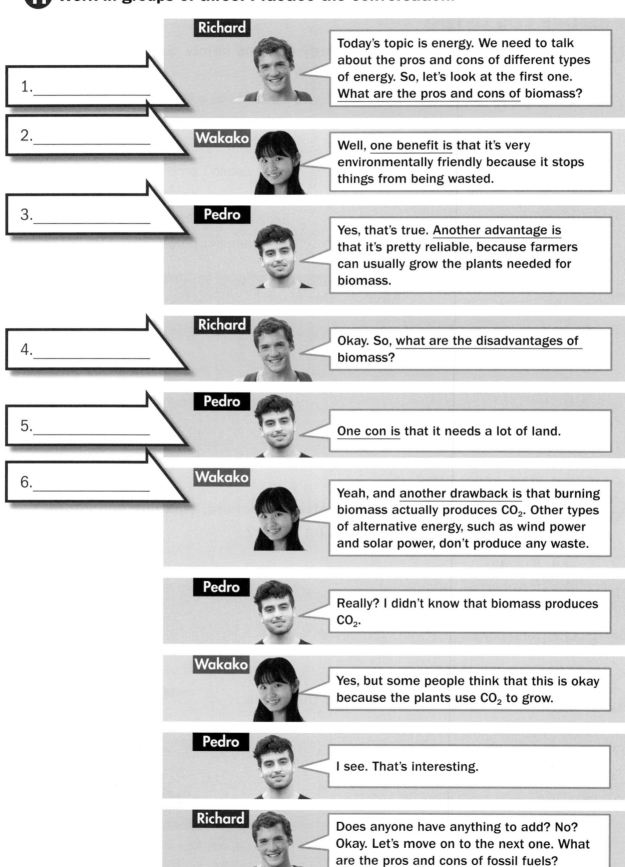

1. _____

Richard

Today's topic is energy. We need to talk about the pros and cons of different types of energy. So, let's look at the first one. What are the pros and cons of biomass?

2. _____

Wakako

Well, one benefit is that it's very environmentally friendly because it stops things from being wasted.

3. _____

Pedro

Yes, that's true. Another advantage is that it's pretty reliable, because farmers can usually grow the plants needed for biomass.

4. _____

Richard

Okay. So, what are the disadvantages of biomass?

5. _____

Pedro

One con is that it needs a lot of land.

6. _____

Wakako

Yeah, and another drawback is that burning biomass actually produces CO_2. Other types of alternative energy, such as wind power and solar power, don't produce any waste.

Pedro

Really? I didn't know that biomass produces CO_2.

Wakako

Yes, but some people think that this is okay because the plants use CO_2 to grow.

Pedro

I see. That's interesting.

Richard

Does anyone have anything to add? No? Okay. Let's move on to the next one. What are the pros and cons of fossil fuels?

DISCUSSION

12 🔊 2-39 **Look at the chart. Add labels to the conversation on page 72. Then practice saying the phrases in the chart.**

💬 **DISCUSSION SKILL:** Discussing the pros and cons of something

Asking about pros and cons	• **What are the pros and cons of** biomass? • **What are the advantages of** wind power? • **What are the disadvantages of** fossil fuels?
Describing the pros	• **The advantages / benefits / pros are** that it's reliable and safe. • **One advantage / benefit / pro is** that it's very environmentally friendly. • **Another advantage / benefit / pro is** that it's pretty reliable.
Describing the cons	• **The disadvantages / drawbacks / cons are** that it's expensive and dangerous. • **One disadvantage / drawback / con is** it needs a lot of land. • **Another disadvantage / drawback / con is** that it produces CO_2.

13 **Work in small groups. Discuss the pros and cons of the energy sources below. Then decide which energy sources Japan should prioritize. Use the phrases in Activity 12 and the diagram below to help you.**

biomass / fossil fuels / hydroelectric power / nuclear power / solar power / wind power

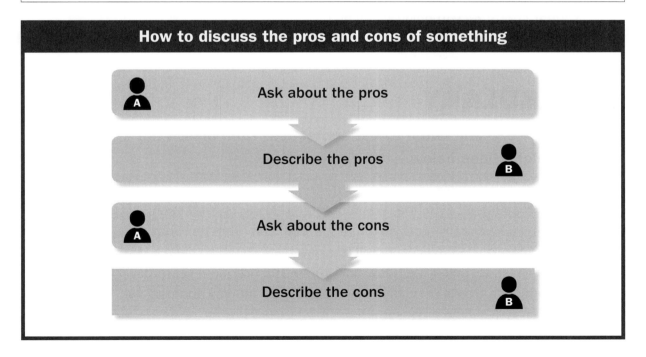

How to discuss the pros and cons of something

A — Ask about the pros

Describe the pros — B

A — Ask about the cons

Describe the cons — B

A: Okay. Today's topic is possible sources of energy for Japan. Let's talk about the first one. What are some of the pros of biomass?

B: Well, one benefit is ...

Equal Pay in Sports

GOAL: Learn how to discuss both sides of an argument

GET READY

1 **Discuss these questions with a partner.**

▷ What sports do you enjoy watching?
▷ Who are some of the richest sports stars in the world?
▷ Do sports stars get paid too much?

VOCABULARY

2 🔊 2-40 **Read and listen to the sentences. Then match the words in bold to the definitions below.**

> **1.** Some sports players **earn** a lot of money. ___
> **2.** Each member of the team is supported **equally** by the coach. ___
> **3.** She worked really hard, so she got **a pay raise** from her boss. ___
> **4.** A lot of people were unhappy with the new team shirts, so there was **a protest**. ___
> **5.** The team **revealed** their new uniform for the first time yesterday. ___
> **6.** The coach **treats** us really well—he's always friendly and positive. ___

a. showed something that was secret
b. behaves towards (someone); interacts with (someone)
c. get money for working
d. in the same way
e. an increase in salary
f. an event when people show they disagree with something

LISTENING

3 🔊 2-41~43 **Read the listening tip. Listen and repeat the example sentences.**

LISTENING TIP: Contractions

In spoken English, we often use contractions instead of full forms.

1. **Full form:** They <u>are not</u> my favorite team.
   Contraction: <u>They're</u> not my favorite team.
2. **Full form:** <u>We have</u> been to the stadium three times.
   Contraction: <u>We've</u> been to the stadium three times.
3. **Full form:** You <u>should not</u> be late for sports practice.
   Contraction: You <u>shouldn't</u> be late for sports practice.

4 🔊 2-44~46 **Listen and write the missing words. Then listen and repeat the sentences.**

1. That _____ a soccer ball; _____ a basketball.
2. Actually, I _____ like soccer because I _____ understand the rules.
3. Today, _____ going to play and _____ going to watch her.

◆ **LISTEN FOR MAIN IDEAS:**

5 🔊 2-47 **Listen and choose the best summary of the speaker's opinion.**

❑ **a.** Male athletes should be paid more than female athletes.
❑ **b.** Male athletes and female athletes should be paid equally.
❑ **c.** Teams should be free to decide how much to pay their players.

◆ **LISTEN FOR DETAILS:**

6 🔊 2-47 **Listen again and choose the correct words to complete the sentences.**

1. The Australian women's soccer team <u>will</u> / <u>won't be</u> paid the same as the men's team.
2. The US women's soccer team <u>are</u> / <u>aren't</u> paid the same as the men's team.
3. Most sports competitions pay <u>the same</u> / <u>different</u> prize money to men and women.
4. Some sports teams pay men more because men's sports are <u>more popular</u> / <u>harder</u>.

Time for Equal Pay?

Australia's women's soccer team will earn the same pay as the men's team after an agreement to pay male and female players equally. Midfielder Elise Kellond-Knight was very happy with the deal. "As a female soccer player, it's what ¹_____ always dreamed of. We always wanted to be treated equally," she said.

However, many female athletes around the world ²_____ treated equally to men. For example, in 2015, it was revealed that the US women's soccer team were paid only 25% of what the men's team earned. After protests, the women's team were given a pay raise, but ³_____ still not paid the same as the male players.

These days most sports competitions give equal prize money to men and women, but many sports teams and sponsors still treat women differently. They argue that women's sports ⁴_____ as popular as men's sports and ⁵_____ make as much money.

But female athletes work just as hard, so ⁶_____ they get the same amount of money?

CONVERSATION

◆ **BEFORE YOU LISTEN:**

8 Look at these sentences. Which ones are reasons for equal pay in sports and which are reasons against equal pay in sports?

	for	against
1. Men are stronger and faster than women.		
2. Paying people equally will encourage more women to become athletes.		
3. More people pay to watch men's sports.		
4. Traditionally, women's sports have not been on TV a lot, but there is growing demand for them.		
5. Men's sports can be tougher or take longer—for example, male tennis players play five sets, whereas women play three.		
6. Women train just as hard as men.		
7. It's important to pay everyone equally if they do the same kind of work, including sports.		
8. The most famous athletes should get the most money for commercials—and male athletes are more famous.		

◆ **LISTEN FOR MAIN IDEAS:**

9 🔊 2-48 Listen to a conversation between Kaoru and Michael. Do they agree or disagree about equal pay in sports?

◆ **LISTEN FOR DETAILS:**

10 🔊 2-48 Listen again. Which reasons from Activity 8 do they discuss?

    1. Against equal pay: _____ _____

    2. For equal pay: _____ _____

11 Work in pairs. Practice the conversation.

Kaoru: So, what do you think, Michael? Should female athletes get paid the same as men?

Explaining one side of the argument and then the other

Michael: Well, on the one hand, it's true that male athletes are generally stronger and faster than women, but on the other hand, female athletes train just as hard. I don't think men should get paid more just because their bodies are different. What do you think?

Kaoru: I agree. As you said, female athletes work just as hard as male athletes. And they're just as skilled, so they should definitely be paid the same.

Michael: So why do men get paid more?

Explaining what some people think

Kaoru: Well, some people say that men should get more money because more people watch men's sports, but I don't think that's fair. Men's sports are on TV more often, so that's why more people watch them. Women's sports are actually very popular too. For example, a lot of people watch the Women's World Cup when it's on TV. If more TV channels showed women's sports, more people would watch them.

Michael: Yeah, I think you're right.

DISCUSSION

12 🔊 2-49 **Look at the chart. Underline the phrases in the conversation on page 78. Then practice saying the phrases in the chart.**

💬 **DISCUSSION SKILL:** Discussing both sides of an argument	
Explaining one side of the argument and then the other	· **On the one hand**, male athletes are generally stronger and faster, **but on the other hand**, female athletes train just as hard. · **Some people think that** men's sports are more exciting because men are stronger and faster, **whereas others think that** women's sports are just as exciting because the players are just as skillful.
Explaining what some people think	· **Some people say that** men should get more money because more people watch men's sports. · **Opponents of** equal pay **think that** men should be paid more because men's sports make more money. · **Supporters of** equal pay **say that** sports clubs should share the money they make between their male and female teams.

13 **Discuss this question with your partner: *Should male and female sports players be paid equally?* Use the phrases in Activity 12 and the diagram below to help you.**

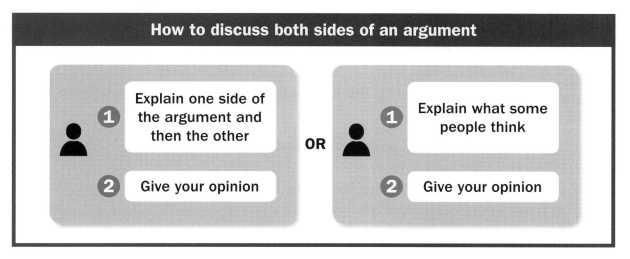

How to discuss both sides of an argument

1 Explain one side of the argument and then the other	OR	1 Explain what some people think
2 Give your opinion		2 Give your opinion

A: Should male and female sports players be paid equally?
B: Well, on the one hand …

Gaming Addiction

GOAL: Learn how to interrupt politely and deal with interruptions

GET READY

1 Discuss these questions with a partner.

▷ How often do you play video games?

▷ How many hours should teenagers play games per day?

▷ Is gaming bad for children and teenagers?

VOCABULARY

2 🔊 2-50 **Read and listen to the sentences. Then match the words in bold to the definitions below.**

1. Some people become **addicted to** drugs or alcohol. ___
2. Students **are not allowed to** use their phones in class. ___
3. Teenagers must come home before **the curfew**. ___
4. The cost of video games has **increased** in the last 10 years. ___
5. The government **introduced** some new rules about video games. ___
6. One hundred people completed **a survey** about their opinions on gaming. ___

a. started using

b. cannot stop using

c. must not

d. a time when people must be at home

e. gone up

f. a list of questions about something

LISTENING

3 🔊 2-51, 52 **Read the listening tip. Listen and repeat the example sentences.**

LISTENING TIP: Linking with _r_

When one word ends in _r_ and the next word starts with a vowel sound, the words link.

1. One hundred people completed a survey about their opinions on gaming.
2. Some people become addicted to drugs or alcohol.

4 🔊 2-53~55 **Listen and write the missing words. Then listen and repeat the sentences.**

1. My computer was slow so I got some more memory _____ __.
2. The _____ ____ children that play games has increased a lot.
3. In our house, the _____ ___ banned after 10 p.m.

◆ **LISTEN FOR MAIN IDEAS:**

5 🔊 2-56 **Listen to the report and choose the best summary.**

❏ **a.** Some members of the Chinese government are addicted to gaming.
❏ **b.** Schools in China are using video games to teach teenagers about addiction.
❏ **c.** There are new rules about playing games for teenagers in China.

◆ **LISTEN FOR DETAILS:**

6 🔊 2-56 **Listen again and choose the correct answers to complete the sentences.**

1. From Monday to Friday, Chinese teenagers are allowed to play video games for …
❏ **a.** 18 minutes per day.
❏ **b.** 90 minutes per day.
❏ **c.** 3 hours per day.

2. People that are addicted to gaming play for …
❏ **a.** 4 to 5 hours per day.
❏ **b.** 7 hours per day.
❏ **c.** 17 hours per day.

3. Experts think people who spend too much time gaming have problems with …
❏ **a.** their weight.
❏ **b.** their behavior.
❏ **c.** their eyes.

China Introduces Gaming Curfew

China has introduced a new rule about online gaming [1]_____ _____ _____. Children and teenagers are not allowed to play online games between 10 p.m. and 8 a.m. Also, they can only play games [2]_____ __ _____ of 90 minutes on weekdays and three hours on the weekend.

The government explained that these new rules will stop young people from becoming addicted to games. A recent survey by China's Ministry of Education found that 17.7% of Chinese teenagers may be addicted to gaming. These teens play games for between [3]_____ _____ _____ hours every day.

Some experts believe that children and teenagers are doing badly at school because they spend too much time playing games. Other experts think that too much gaming is bad for [4]_____ _____, and that it has increased the number of children that need glasses.

CONVERSATION

◆ BEFORE YOU LISTEN:

8 Look at these sentences. Check (✓) the sentences you agree with. Compare your opinions with your partner.

❑ **1.** Playing video games is a good way to relax.

❑ **2.** People who play a lot of video games get bad grades.

❑ **3.** Playing video games can help people learn about the world.

❑ **4.** Playing video games late at night stops people sleeping.

❑ **5.** Looking at a screen all day is bad for your eyes.

❑ **6.** Kids play video games as their parents are too busy to play with them.

❑ **7.** It's dangerous for young children to play online games.

❑ **8.** Playing video games teaches people useful skills.

❑ **9.** Teenagers who play video games are less likely to behave badly.

❑ **10.** The government should not decide what people do in their free time.

◆ LISTEN FOR MAIN IDEAS:

9 🔊 2-57 **Listen to a conversation between Jane and Yoshi. Does Yoshi think that a gaming curfew is a good idea?**

❑ **a.** Yes, he does.

❑ **b.** No, he doesn't.

❑ **c.** He's not sure.

◆ LISTEN FOR DETAILS:

10 🔊 2-57 **Listen again. What does Yoshi think?**

❑ **a.** Most children don't play a lot of games.

❑ **b.** The government should set rules about the number of hours children play.

❑ **c.** Children's parents should make rules about how long they can play for.

11 Work in pairs. Practice the conversation.

Jane: So, do you think a video game curfew is a good idea?

Yoshi: Uh, I'm not sure. I mean, I think it's important that children don't play too many games but—

Interrupting politely

Jane: Sorry, but can I just add something?

Accepting the interruption

Yoshi: Sure. Go ahead.

Jane: I don't think all games are bad. Games can be a good way to learn things.

Continuing after the interruption

Yoshi: Yes, that's a great point. Anyway, as I was saying, it's important that children don't play too many games, but it doesn't seem fair to set strict rules like this. I think—

Interrupting politely

Jane: Sorry to interrupt again, but can I say something?

Rejecting the interruption

Yoshi: Actually, can I just finish what I was saying first?

Jane: Yes, sorry.

Continuing after the interruption

Yoshi: Getting back to what I was saying, I think that parents should decide how many hours their children can play for.

Jane: I agree. I think parents know if their children have done their homework or not.

DISCUSSION

12 🔊 2-58 **Look at the chart. Underline the phrases that Jane and Yoshi use in the conversation on page 84. Then practice saying the phrases in the chart.**

💬 **DISCUSSION SKILL:** Interrupting politely and dealing with interruptions	
Interrupting politely	· Sorry to interrupt, but can I say something? · Sorry, but can I just add something?
Accepting the interruption	· Sure. · Go ahead.
Rejecting the interruption	· Actually, can I just finish what I was saying first? · In a moment. I'd like to finish my point first.
Continuing after the interruption	· As I was saying, ... · Getting back to what I was saying, ...

13 **Discuss this question with your partner:** *Do you think a video game curfew is a good idea?* **Use the phrases in Activity 12 and the diagram below to help you.**

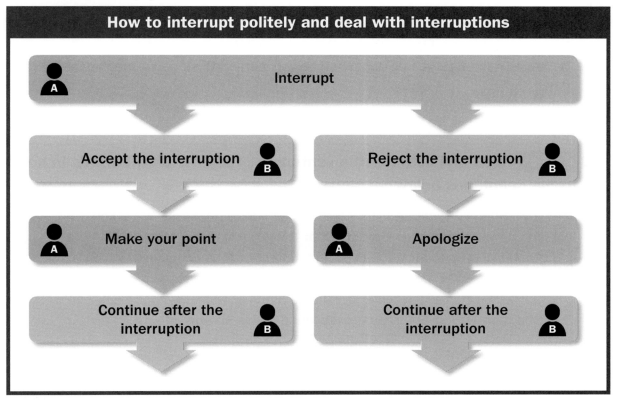

How to interrupt politely and deal with interruptions

Interrupt — A

Accept the interruption — B   Reject the interruption — B

Make your point — A   Apologize — A

Continue after the interruption — B   Continue after the interruption — B

A: Do you think a video game curfew is a good idea?
B: Hmm. I think ...

Unit 15
Britain's Royal Family

GOAL: Learn how to summarize a discussion

GET READY

1 **Discuss these questions with a partner.**

▷ Which members of the British Royal Family do you know?
▷ Are you interested in the British Royal Family? Why?/Why not?
▷ What kinds of stories do Japanese newspapers publish about the Japanese Royal Family?

VOCABULARY

2 🔊 2-59 **Read and listen to the sentences. Then match the words in bold to the definitions below.**

> **1.** Some people think that the Royal Family doesn't **deserve** to be rich. ___
> **2.** Repairs to the palace are **funded** by the government. ___
> **3.** Prince William is a very **high-profile** member of the British Royal Family. ___
> **4.** **The press** writes about the Royal Family as people like reading about them. ___
> **5.** Some members of **the public** love the Royal Family, whereas other people don't. ___
> **6.** She **quit** her job at the palace because it was so stressful. ___

a. ordinary people
b. left
c. famous and often in the news
d. paid for
e. should have something because of hard work
f. the news media, especially newspapers

LISTENING

3 🔊 2-60, 61 **Read the listening tip. Listen and repeat the example sentences.**

> **LISTENING TIP: Linking similar sounds**
>
> **When one word ends with a similar sound to the next word, it often sounds like there is only one sound.**
>
> **1.** She quit her job at the palace because it wa(s) so stressful.
> **2.** Some people think tha(t) the Royal Family doesn'(t) deserve to be rich.

4 🔊 2-62~64 **Listen and write the missing words. Then listen and repeat the sentences.**

1. They explained _____ _____ to the press.

2. The _____ _____ a long story about them.

3. The next day, the _____ _____ out before lunch.

◆ LISTEN FOR MAIN IDEAS:

5 🔊 2-65 **Listen to a report about Prince Harry and Meghan Markle quitting the British Royal Family. Choose the correct sentence.**

❑ **a.** The speaker thinks that this is bad news for the Royal Family.

❑ **b.** The speaker thinks that this is good news for the Royal Family.

❑ **c.** The speaker does not give an opinion about whether this is good or bad news for the Royal Family.

◆ LISTEN FOR DETAILS:

6 🔊 2-65 **Listen again and decide if each sentence is true or false.**

1. Harry and Meghan said that they quit the Royal Family because they were unhappy with Harry's family.   T / F

2. Almost £30 million is given to the Royal Family by the government each year.   T / F

3. The Royal Family is very useful for the tourism industry in the UK.   T / F

Leaving the Royal Family

In January 2020, Prince Harry and Meghan Markle shocked the world by quitting the British Royal Family. Their reason was ¹_____ _____ wanted more privacy from the press. This is understandable since Prince Harry's mother, Princess Diana, died in a car crash after being chased by the paparazzi when Harry was ²_____ _____ years old.

However, many people argue that media attention is part of the job ³_____ _____ Family members. After all, they are funded by the public. In fact, almost £300 million ⁴__ _____ on the Royal Family each year—to pay for things like travel, events, and security.

Although ⁵_____ _____ like a lot of money, the Royal Family actually makes £1.8 billion for the UK each year by helping to promote it as an attractive tourist destination and a desirable country to trade with.

So, do members of the Royal Family deserve more privacy? Harry and Meghan clearly thought so, and the UK has now ⁶_____ _____ of its highest-profile spokespersons.

CONVERSATION

◆ **BEFORE YOU LISTEN:**

8 Read the quotes and check (✓) the ones that support the Royal Family's right to privacy.

❑ **1.** "Newspapers should only print important news—and gossip is not important."

❑ **2.** "Nobody believes what they read in the newspapers anyway."

❑ **3.** "It doesn't matter if you're rich or famous. It hurts when people tell lies about you."

❑ **4.** "People forget that they didn't choose to be famous."

❑ **5.** "Losing privacy is the price of being famous."

❑ **6.** "People have the right to know about the bad behavior of princes and princesses."

◆ **LISTEN FOR MAIN IDEAS:**

9 🔊 2-66 Listen to the conversation between Emi, Lukas, and Hannah. Do they think the Royal Family has a right to privacy?

1. Lukas: yes / no / doesn't say

2. Hannah: yes / no / doesn't say

3. Emi: yes / no / doesn't say

◆ **LISTEN FOR DETAILS:**

10 🔊 2-66 Listen again and choose the correct words to complete the sentences.

1. Lukas thinks famous people <u>deserve</u> / <u>don't deserve</u> to have some time off.

2. Hannah thinks that famous people <u>like</u> / <u>should expect</u> newspapers to write about them.

3. Lukas says that newspapers write a lot of <u>false</u> / <u>personal</u> stories about famous people.

4. Hannah says that it's <u>okay</u> / <u>not okay</u> for newspapers to write untrue stories.

11 **Work in groups of three. Practice the conversation.**

Emi: So, let's start with the first question: Do members of the Royal Family deserve more privacy? Lukas, what do you think?

Lukas: I think they do. It's not fair to follow them everywhere or write about their private lives. I know people are interested in them, but they should be able to have some free time too.

Emi: Do you agree, Hannah?

Hannah: I'm not sure. If someone is rich and famous, they should know that people like reading stories about them. Losing privacy is the price of being famous.

Lukas: But newspapers publish a lot of gossip and false information about famous people. It's not fair to the people they're writing about.

Introducing the summary

Summarizing the key points

Checking the summary

Emi: Okay. So, let me summarize our discussion so far. Lukas thinks that newspapers shouldn't write stories about the private lives of famous people, including the Royal Family. However, Hannah believes that the price of being famous is having people write stories about you. Is that correct?

Hannah: Yes, but I want to add that I don't think that newspapers should write untrue stories about famous people. Unfortunately, that's what happens and it's impossible to change.

Emi: Okay. So, now let's move on to the next question ...

DISCUSSION

12 🔊 2-67 **Underline the phrases from the chart in the conversation on page 90. Then practice saying the phrases in the chart.**

💬 DISCUSSION SKILL: Summarizing a discussion	
Introducing the summary	· **So, let me summarize our discussion (so far).** · **I'd like to summarize our thoughts about this question.**
Summarizing the key points	· Lukas **thinks that** newspapers shouldn't write stories about people's private lives. · **We agree that** newspapers shouldn't publish untrue stories. · **Most people think that** the Royal Family deserves privacy. · **Some people believe that** it's okay to write gossip about famous people.
Checking the summary	· **Is that correct?** · **Does anyone want to add anything?**

13 **Work in small groups. Discuss the questions below. Take turns leading the discussion. Use the phrases in Activity 12 and the diagram below to help you.**

· Does the Royal Family have a right to privacy?
· Should the Royal Family receive money from the government?
· Is the Royal Family useful for the country?

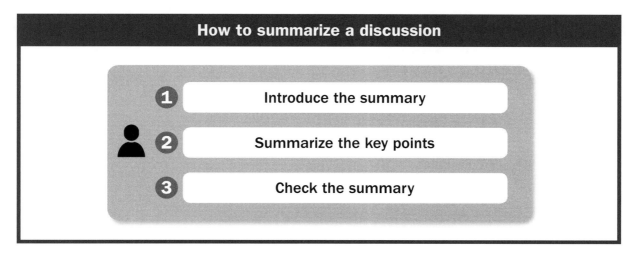

How to summarize a discussion

1. Introduce the summary
2. Summarize the key points
3. Check the summary

A: *Today's topic is the Royal Family. Let's start with the first question. Does the Royal Family have a right to privacy?*
B: *That's a difficult question. I think that ...*

TEXT PRODUCTION STAFF

edited by	編集
Eiichi Tamura	田村 栄一
Taiichi Sano	佐野 泰一

cover design by	表紙デザイン
Nobuyoshi Fujino	藤野 伸芳

text design by	本文デザイン
ALIUS(Hiroyuki Kinouchi)	アリウス（木野内宏行）

In partnership with	制作協力
GLOBAL BRIDGE	グローバルブリッジ

CD PRODUCTION STAFF

recorded by	吹き込み者
Dominic Allen (AmE)	ドミニク・アレン（アメリカ英語）
Jeffrey Rowe (CanE)	ジェフリー・ロウ（カナダ英語）
Jenny Shima (AmE)	ジェニー・シマ（アメリカ英語）
Lisa Fujiwara (AmE)	リサ・フジワラ（アメリカ英語）

Global Issues —An Introduction to Discussion Skills—
身近な世界を英語で発信

2021年1月20日　初版発行
2024年4月10日　第5刷発行

著　者　Garry Pearson
　　　　Graham Skerritt
　　　　Adrian Francis
　　　　吉塚 弘

発 行 者　佐野 英一郎
発 行 所　株式会社 成美堂
　　　　〒101-0052　東京都千代田区神田小川町3-22
　　　　TEL 03-3291-2261　FAX 03-3293-5490
　　　　https://www.seibido.co.jp

印 刷・製 本　（株）萩原印刷

ISBN 978-4-7919-7225-8　　　　　　　　　　Printed in Japan